The Last Hussar

By Peter Stephaich

Hamilton Books
An Imprint of
Rowman & Littlefield
Lanham • Boulder • New York • Toronto • Plymouth, UK

**Copyright © 2017 by
Hamilton Books**
4501 Forbes Boulevard
Suite 200
Lanham, Maryland 20706
Hamilton Books Acquisitions Department (301) 459-3366

Unit A, Whitacre Mews, 26-34 Stannary Street,
London SE11 4AB, United Kingdom

British Library Cataloging in Publication Information Available

Library of Congress Control Number: 2016958685
ISBN: 978-0-7618-6868-2 (pbk : alk. paper)
eISBN: 978-0-7618-6869-9

For

Louise and the "4 P's" –

Peter, Paul, Peggy, and Pauline

Introduction

When I was eleven years old, my mother told me that Cousin Louise Hitchcock was coming to lunch and was bringing her fiancé. I asked who Louise was about to marry, and Mother replied, "I can't pronounce his name, but he's the best-looking man I've ever seen." That aroused my curiosity, and when Louise walked in with her beau, I recognized at once that he was like no one I had met before. The man who bent down to shake my hand was exceptionally tall, with fine manly features, and a warm ingratiating smile. But what immediately impressed me was that he spoke and moved with an effortless elegance that I was not accustomed to. He was obviously not an American. It turned out that his name was Peter Stephaich, and my first encounter with him proved to be the beginning of a friendship which has lasted more than fifty years.

In 1962, Peter and Louise joined me on a month-long safari in Tanzania, and it was then that Peter began to tell me about his extraordinary journey through life. He had grown up on his family's estate in rural Hungary, where the necessities of life were raised in his father's fields, where his ancestors lay buried in the local church, and where there was a reassuring continuity between past and present. His family belonged to the landed gentry and mingled easily with the historic Hungarian families. He came from a gracious world of country living – of horses, hunting dogs, and pheasant shoots – where family ties were sacred and people lived in life-giving proximity to the earth – a peaceful, structured, comfortable world where one had time to think about life and could live graciously – a world where life itself had become art.

From the reassuring certainties of his youth, Peter was suddenly and ruthlessly expelled by World War II. The young man who had never shot more than the wild game of his county found himself at war with Soviet Russia. At one point, his group of refugees was living in a cellar and eating cuts of meat from a dead horse that lay in the snow. And when the conflict ended, his land was confiscated, his country communized, and his family reduced to poverty.

But Peter has survived every calamity, and, more to the point, he has done so with style. A talent for finding hidden treasure in adversity is certainly one of his most admirable qualities. In a long and eventful life, which could be graphed as a series of deep plunges and steep recoveries, Peter has learned to make the most out of today, because tomorrow could not be counted on. He has been quick to recognize what is good in life, to cling to it, and to retrieve it, when misfortune swept it away.

In the elaborately formal bird shoots which he labored to perfect and promote, Peter caught glimpses of the refined, rarefied Europe that he had known in his youth and had come to idealize. He gloried in the ritual occasions when men and women shot with firearms that were custom-made works of art – when traditional standards of conduct and attire were strictly and cheerfully adhered to. He loved the sumptuous concluding banquet that followed the shoot and reflected centuries of effort and refinement in every detail – where the guests wore evening dress, the food and wines were exquisite, and the servants impeccably trained; where the ceremonial meal in the storied

Shooting skeet with cousin Jay Mellon, near Paris, 1961

castle would end with cognac, port, the finest cigars, and with parlor games played beside roaring fireplaces on long winter nights. Perhaps most of all, he treasured the lifelong friendships that were formed by sharing these experiences. What Peter loves is civilization. If he had settled in America, he would have aged twenty years in one year.

Just as paint and clay are meaningless materials, until the artist fashions them into something beautiful, so life itself is also meaningless until we give it a form that arouses our delight and admiration. A passionate European, Peter has never faltered in his longing to give form and beauty to life. And while we cannot any longer do this precisely as he wanted to, we can take inspiration from his ideal. We can make it our guiding star and then follow it in new directions.

Above all, Peter has been a loyal and delightful companion to those who were favored with his friendship. There is much that we can learn from such a man!

James Mellon, 2009

At the urging of P-3 and P-4 and with the help of Louise, I begin my story. I never kept a diary or made notes, and any confusion of names and dates is a logical consequence of my age.

Your punishment, my dear sons and daughters, is that I ask you to read these pages, whatever they may be worth. Please understand that I will have to make frequent digressions into European history because it affected my life so profoundly.

Here I go. Listen, Peter, Paul, Peggy and Pauline:

I

The World into Which I Came

I was born on June 3, 1920, in Kaposvár, Hungary, one day before the tragic Treaty of Trianon, whereby Hungary lost 71 percent of its territory and 63 percent of its population to the Little Entente. The Little Entente consisted of:

Czechoslovakia

After World War I, Tomás Masaryk, a clever politician and a friend of President Woodrow Wilson, convinced the victorious Allied Powers to form Bohemia, Moravia, and Slovakia into a single republic. It came to be named Czechoslovakia, and Masaryk was elected its first president. The problem for Hungarians was that Slovakia had belongs to Hungary for nine hundred years.

Romania

This country was created in 1880, when Britain, France and Russia recognized its independence and approved the enthronement of a German prince, Karl von Hohenzollern-

Map of old Hungary

Sigmaringen, as King of Romania. His daughter-in-law, later Queen Marie, was a granddaughter of Britain's Queen Victoria. She was attractive and obviously well connected. In 1919, she also became a patriot by taking a number of Romanian beauties to Paris for the peace conference at Versailles. That helped! Transylvania, which had belonged to Hungary for a thousand years, was given to Romania.

Yugoslavia

At the Versailles Conference, in 1919, the victorious Allied Powers created the Kingdom of the Serbs, Croats and Slovenes and recognized the Karageorgevich dynasty as its royal family. Catholic Croatia, however, had belonged to Hungary for eight hundred years but was included in this new kingdom.

Four historic dynasties were dethroned after World War I: the Habsburg emperors of Austria and kings of Hungary, the Hohenzollern kings of Prussia and German emperors, the czars of Russia, and the Ottoman sultans of Turkey. All of these countries became republics, which created a vacuum of power in Europe and led to disastrous political, economic, and social disorder.

Hungary's defeat in World War I resulted in the immediate dissolution of our union with Austria. The Habsburg monarch, King Charles, who had reigned over both countries, went into exile but did not abdicate. In 1919, the communist leader, Béla Kun, briefly seized power and unleashed a program in which hundreds of middle and upper class Hungarians were murdered. Known as the "Red Terror," this wave of violence instilled a deep and lasting fear of communism in most Hungarians. That Kun was in fact a Transylvanian Jew named Cohen falsely linked our numerous Jewish minority to communism and unfortunately strengthened Hungarian anti-Semitism immeasurably. Béla Kun's brutal and chaotic misrule was however quickly ended by moderate and right-wing forces, some of them led by a hero of World War I, Admiral Miklós Horthy (pronounced "MeeKLÓSH Horty"). The Hungarian parliment was then summoned to devise a new system of government for our country.

The Allied Powers and the Little Entente were vehemently opposed to restoring the Habsburg monarchy, and Hungarians themselves were deeply divided over whether their king should be recalled from exile. As a compromise, our parliament decided that Hungary would remain a kingdom, but in the king's absence the royal powers would be exercised by a regent. Admiral Horthy was then installed as Regent of Hungary with the flowery title of "His Serene Highness." He became our acting chief-of-state, also our military commander-in-chief, and from 1920 to 1944 he was the dominant figure in our country's political life.

Horthy had ruled for only three months when the victorious Allied Powers forced him to approve the hated Treaty of Trianon. Little wonder that he spent the remaining years of his regency dreaming and scheming to regain the territories that Britain, France, and America had vengefully taken from Hungary and awarded to the Little Entente. In this effort, all of Hungary stood behind him. That the Regent was also an implacable opponent of communism both at home and abroad further enhanced his popularity.

But Horthy could also be vain and self-serving. He had wrested from our parliment the right to appoint and dismiss prime ministers and to remove whole governments from office. He loved the inflated splendor of his quasi-royal position and was prepared to make ethical compromises to retain it. He had always been a monarchist, but when King Charles and Queen Zita attempted to return from exile uninvited, Horthy ordered Hungarian soldiers to shoot at their train, then had them arrested and deported.

The Treaty of Versailles, which the Allied Powers imposed on Germany at the end of World War I, was far too harsh. Sixty percent of the German population came to be unemployed, and inflation reached catastrophic proportions. When a man appeared who shouted, "I will give you work, I will stabilize the currency, and I will unite all the Germanic peoples in one enormous Reich," the Germans thundered, "Heil Hitler!"

The winners of World War I were England, with Prime Minister Lloyd George; France with Premier Georges Clemenceau, who detested the Catholic and aristocratic Austro-Hungarian Empire and had done all he could to destroy our Habsburg monarchy; and the U.S.A., with President Woodrow Wilson. These leaders were all Freemasons. In the Austro-Hungarian Empire, Freemasonry and other secret organizations had long been forbidden.

France had been an ally of Russia since the Congress of Vienna, in 1815. But Germany eventually became the leading European power, after Bismarck crushingly defeated the French and Austro-Hungarian empires. Symbolically, the German Empire, or Reich, was founded by Bismarck, not in Germany but in conquered France, at Versailles.

After 1871, three mighty powers remained in the Old World: England, which ruled an empire on which the sun never set and whose navy controlled all of the world's oceans; a united Germany, ruled by the King of Prussia, who was also the German Emperor, and Czarist Russia, still a primitive but immense autocratic empire, which continually plotted to extend its influence into Europe – in the North on the Baltic, in the South on the Black Sea and on the Mediterranean.

Such was the historical background of the world into which I was born. As to the history of our family, permit me to give you a brief résumé.

Origin of the Stephaich Family

Our male ancestral line originated in Croatia, which was part of Hungary from the twelfth century until the end of World War I.

Long ago, family names did not exist, and Stephaich simply meant "son of Stephen". Our coat of arms, which features a unicorn, was the same in Croatia during the fifteenth century as in Hungary later on. As the Turks were advancing through the Balkans, old man Stephaich came to Hungary and settled in the county of Somogy. Rudolph II of Habsburg, King of Hungary, confirmed the Croatian nobility in 1608. So we are true Hungarians since that date.

It is interesting how names originate. The well-known family of Thyssen Bornemisza de Kaszon started because a man in the village of Kaszon did not drink wine. So they called him Bor-nem-isza, or "wine-no-drinker". The famous German steel magnate Baron Thyssen married a Hungarian "wine-no-drinker".

The position the Stephaich family occupied in traditional Hungarian society is important and calls for some explanation. We were a noble landed family in the county of Somogy from at least 1608 until World War II. In old Hungary, only members of the nobility could serve as army officers, vote in elections, or hold important political positions. Until 1848, nobles were not even taxed. Our Stephaich ancestors enjoyed all of these privileges and were always at home on the top level of Hungarian society. That some noble families came to be titled and others did not was less important than a foreigner might imagine.

Actually, our family did produce one titled individual: I refer to Major General Baron Ferenc Stephaich de Nemes-Déd, who

Major General Baron Ferenc Stephaich de Nemes-Déd, 1739-1811

Our coat of arms

Note the head of a decapitated Turk

was born in 1739 and died on April 9, 1811. In *The Military Order of (Empress) Maria Theresia*, published in 1857 by J. Hirtenfeld (see pages 414 and 415), it is recorded that for his gallantry in the Seven Years' War against King Frederick "the Great" of Prussia, Ferenc Stephaich de Nemes-Déd, who is described as "of noble origin," was admitted to the abovementioned order and was awarded a hereditary barony in the Hungarian peerage, having already attained the rank of major general for extraordinary services rendered. However, if the surviving records are reliable, I am not descended from this relative, and the refusal of every member of our family to use his title suggests that any male lines that may have descended from him have extinguished.

Our Grandparents

My paternal grandparents were Pál Stephaich (1861-1942) and Mária de Gombos (1865-1916). Grandfather was called Pipás ("Piper") because he smoked a pipe all day. His widowed mother, born Mária de Thassy, was quite wealthy and owned estates in various parts of our beloved county, Somogy. So it's not surprising that my grandfather lived in the country all his life.

During the shooting season, he would ride in a carriage from one estate to another. He smoked various large pipes, and when he went somewhere, he would say that his destination was one pipeload or two pipeloads away. After every luncheon or dinner, he would smoke a Turkish "tshibuk," a pipe with a very long stem. It took him about an hour to smoke this pipe, and during that time he could do nothing else. We would ask him, "Grandfather, what are you thinking about, when you sit smoking in your armchair?" "I'm talking to God" would be his answer. He played the piano well, always with his pipe in his mouth.

As a young man of about twenty, he had jumped over a ditch during a duck shoot and had failed to notice that some mud had got jammed into the barrels of his shotgun. The next time he fired the gun it exploded. The blast ruptured his eardrums, and he became almost deaf in both ears. From then on, he would shoot with a brown German retriever, named Pick. The dog would sit in front of him, and he would watch the dog closely. Whenever the dog suddenly turned his head, he knew a bird was coming, and he would shoot it with his 20-gauge gun. He kept a game book, in which he recorded the date, the number, and the quality of the game, the direction of the wind, and the names of the other hunters, or "Guns". One time, we added up the number of pheasants, partridges, hares, and other game animals he had shot. The total came to over 50,000. Not bad for a handicapped man.

As children, we loved to hear Grandfather tell stories. One time, he told us about arriving in a village where there was a Protestant church. These churches had a cockerel on top of the bell tower instead of a cross. That day there was great excitement in the village square. Some men were trying to remove the cockerel because it had become loose and might fall, but they couldn't disconnect it. Grandfather, who had all kinds of guns in his carriage, seized a rifle and with a couple of well-aimed bullets shot down the cockerel, to thunderous cheering from the villagers.

Grandfather was very kind, amusing, fun-loving, and a good Christian, but he had a facility for understanding only what he wanted to. He was loved by everyone and died at the age of eighty-two – with his pipe in his mouth.

There could not have been a greater contrast than between my two grandfathers. My mother's father, Alajos Kladnigg (1867-1942), was an Austrian engineer who came to Hungary long before World War I and decided to build a sugar factory at Kaposvár, the capital of Somogy. He was a hard-working intelligent man who had few interests apart from his family and his profession. He normally succeeded at whatever he did, and many of the Hungarian gentry came to envy him.

My maternal grandfather, Alajos Kladnigg, 1867-1942

But Grandfather Kladnigg was very unlucky with his children. He and his wife, Johanna Sedlmayr (1867-1947) had only one son, an invalid from the age of eighteen until his death in old age. Three little daughters died of diphtheria, which in those days was usually fatal. All his affection was therefore concentrated on his only surviving child, our mother, Theodóra, or "Dóra", as she was called.

Grandmother Kladnigg was the most lovable, charming woman, and she and our grandfather were madly in love all their lives. Grandmother adored music and played the piano beautifully. She used to dance alone around the dining table after she had locked the doors. Once a year, chaperoned by a friend, she would go to Budapest to shop. She bought everything she liked without asking the price. "Just send the bill to my husband," she would say. Grandmother had no idea of money, and she did not want to learn. Once Grandfather asked her, "Couldn't our household do with a pig that weighed 200 kilos less? Wouldn't that give enough sausages?" Grandmother asked, "What is the problem?" When Grandfather replied that he could sell the oversized pig, Grandmother got quite angry and said, "I hope you are not a pig merchant behind my back!" Grandfather gave up.

As a result of Grandfather's hard work and the consequent success of his company, which was partly owned by the Austrian Rothschild family, he became quite wealthy and was able to buy an estate of about 800 acres at Széntgaloskér (unpronounceable, so we just called it "Kér"). It had a twelve-bedroom country house, where we spent our summer holidays. In 1942, I had the luck to inherit what remained of this estate. It was promptly stolen from me by the communist regime, but that is still the only home I have ever owned.

We children had a wonderful time in the country. The house servants and farmhands loved to spoil us. These families worked

Our country house, "Kér," where I grew up

for us all their lives. They thought of our estate as their home and of us children as their little "masters" and "mistresses", as in the American South before the Civil War.

Every winter, when the ponds were frozen, people would cut ice for the large icehouse in our cellar. On one layer of ice they would lay meat – pork, beef, veal, and poultry – then another layer of ice, then different varieties of game – pheasants, partridges, and hares. In the summer, somebody had to go to the icehouse every day because, with the house servants included, there were often twenty people to feed at every meal. When another eight showed up unexpectedly, we would kill a pig or calf or some poultry. There was always plenty to eat from the produce of the estate.

Here is a little story that illustrates the moral standards of that day. Grandfather Kladnigg was a director of the bank in Kaposvár. During the Great Depression, the bank went broke. Since many of Grandfather's employees had accounts in that bank because of his being a director, he felt duty-bound to repay, from his own pocket, the monies they would otherwise have lost.

We children were expected to become multilingual. In the summers, we always had guests from abroad, boys and girls, young and old, Britons, Austrians, Belgians, and Italians. So we picked up foreign languages rather effortlessly at an early age.

We were extremely thankful to Grandfather for sending my sister, Irmi, to school for four years at the academy of the Sacré Coeur in Pressbaum, near Vienna. He had also sent our mother to study there. Irmi cried when she left home, and cried again when she left the school.

I myself was put through one of the most prestigious boys' schools in Vienna, the Theresianum, at Grandfather's expense. Founded by our queen, Maria Theresia, in the eighteenth century, this academy had been awarded a gift of 20,000 acres in Hungary, from which to fund scholarships for the sons of impoverished Hungarian nobility. But my father did not allow me to go as a scholarship student, because we were able to pay the tuition.

Morale de l'histoire: After the debacle of 1939 to '45, the world that our family had known came to an end, and all the material advantages we had enjoyed were swept away. But whatever we had gained by way of education during our youth, thanks to Grandfather Kladnigg's generosity, no power on earth could take away from us, and it served us well in our new life as refugees and later as immigrants.

Grandfather built a church in Kaposvár, where he and our beloved grandmother lie buried in front of the main altar. There is a large window dedicated to Mother and Grandmother in the same church. May these memorials remain there for generations to come.

Our Parents

My father, Pál Stephaich (1887-1966) lived for his family and his estate. He was a good rider, a good shot, and thoroughly enjoyed all the pleasures of country life. When I was a boy, he

Mother

Father

gave me my first shotgun and taught me how to handle it, and I would accompany him on his weekend shoots every Sunday. Father's interests included stock breeding, and I remember that he would import thoroughbred brewery horses from Belgium and Holstein cattle from the Netherlands. He was a college-educated man who had obtained a bachelor's degree from the Royal University of Saint Elizabeth, at Pécs, where I would later study.

In old Hungary, the socially prominent or *comme il faut* occupations for men of our background were the Foreign Office, a commission in one of the prestigious cavalry regiments, a career in the Church, or a position in the government. My father was a lifelong participant in local politics and was popular for his liberal views. Government officials were chosen by vote, and the county executive was elected for a term of ten years. In Somogy, our clan was well represented in government, since my father was twice elected county executive, and before him the same position had been held by the father of my brother-in-law and still earlier by his father-in-law. Our family and its in-laws were leaders in Somogy for a hundred years, and the county came to be known as a little "kingdom within the kingdom".

At the outset of World War II, when the Germans and Russians overran Poland, my father and his friend Monsignor Béla Varga took the lead in establishing schools for Polish refugees who fled to Hungary. Toward the end of the war, Father became a political prisoner of the Hungarian fascists, or Arrow Cross Party, and later he was also imprisoned in a communist concentration camp. Our house and farmland were confiscated. My parents lost all their worldly possessions, and so did my sister, her husband, and their children.

Things got better in Hungary after the Revolution of 1956, and eventually every member of my family came to visit us in France – but not all at the same time. Some family members had to stay in Hungary to reassure our communist government that the travelers would return.

In 1966, while visiting Louise and me in Paris, Father got sick and was flown back to Hungary with my sister. He never considered living anywhere except in his own country. He wanted to die at home, and he did.

Born Theodóra Kladnigg (1894-1984), my mother received a classical education at the academy of the Sacré Coeur, where my sister, Irmi, would also study, later on. She learned languages, the piano, and how to run a household. In the 1930s, she became the head of the Red Cross in Somogy County and was honorary president of various charitable organizations. When World War II broke out, she became a nurse at different hospitals. She was deeply religious. We had to go to church at 7 A.M. before joining Father on his Sunday bird shoots.

After her perilous escape from Hungary during the Revolution of 1956 – a subject I will return to – my mother lived with us in New York, where Louise generously gave her an apartment. Eventually, she came to live with me in Paris, at 54 avenue d'Iéna, which has now been my home for more than fifty years. In 1984, shortly before her ninetieth birthday, my mother died without suffering. Her three children were with her. She lies buried in Kaposvár.

Paul

My only brother, Paul – Pál in Hungarian – was born in 1916 and is four years older than I. Having studied at universities in England, France, and Austria, he had a more diversified and better education than I did. He speaks, reads, and writes seven languages. Like me, Paul embarked on a diplomatic career. He served at our embassy in Rome until 1943 with a dear friend,

My grandfather, my father and my brother, all named Paul (Pál) Stephaich

Hubert Pallavicini, who remained there, at the Vatican, and made a career in the Order of Malta.

During the last years of World War II, Paul served as vice-consul at our consulate in Vienna. For a while, he was able to help feed a large number of refugees by bringing food from our estate in his diplomatic car. He also helped a number of the VIP prisoners in the concentration camp of Dachau by supplying passports to those who needed them desperately. In April 1945, when Russian troops were approaching Vienna, Paul escaped to Switzerland, but he was able to return the following year, and I helped him to resume his diplomatic career as first secretary of the Hungarian Embassy in Prague.

Paul is an excellent bridge player and has taken part in shoots on five continents. For the last fifty years, he has lived in Brazil, and still enjoys good health. He has always been my best friend. Never, in all our lives, have we had a misunderstanding.

Irmi

Born in 1918, my sister, Mária, whom we call "Irmi", is two years older than I. After attending the academy of the Sacré Coeur at Pressbaum, she married our neighbor, Gyula Kacskovics, who was a landowner and a gentleman but was nineteen years older than she. Irmi was not in love with him, but their marriage proved to be a happy one, and it lasted.

After the communist takeover, Irmi, her husband, and our parents were in jail, off and on. She and her three sons were evicted from their home in the country, and in 1951 she had to begin life again, in Budapest. For years, she lived with her sons in a one-room apartment, doing manual labor, as she was a "class enemy" in the communist jargon and was barred from getting a decent job. Her little boys had to walk for one hour every day to get to school. She put all her love, affection, and energy into bringing them up. More than fifty years later, they still worship her, and all three of them and her other fifteen descendants could not be more affectionate or grateful to their mother, grandmother, and

My sister, Irmi, falconing in Hungary

great-grandmother. She inherited all the wonderful qualities of our mother and Grandmother Kladnigg. To know her is both a pleasure and an honor.

My Early Life

I will spare you the details of how I shot my first sparrow. Let me begin with the most important event of my youth. When I was only fifteen, I fell head-over-heels in love with a charming and gorgeous Austrian girl named Annelie Kupelwieser. She was blond and blue-eyed, thin and willowy. I found her incredibly attractive. She had come to stay with us in the country and was teaching French to my sister. She taught me a few things, as well.

Annelie came from a very substantial Viennese family. Her sister had married the leading Austrian industrialist, and her family owned, among other things, the island of Brioni, near the Croatian coast. In the 1920s and early '30s, Brioni was the meeting place of the Central and Eastern European aristocracy, playboys, the wealthy, and people who were just out for fun. Polo, golf, lovely villas, and beaches were all available. Prince Franzi Hohenlohe was in charge of the polo, and the Duke of Spoleto, a member of the Italian royal family, was the social monarch of the island. He had even been offered the crown of Croatia, but after taking a good look at Zagreb had said, "No, thank you." He had proposed marriage to Millicent Rogers, the ravishing mother of my friend Peter Salm, but Mr. Rogers had also said, "No, thank you."

The Kupelwieser family did not charge their innumerable friends for staying on Brioni. In fact, they were so generous that they eventually lost everything, including their island, which in time became the summer retreat of the Yugoslav dictator, Marshal Tito.

Thanks to my maternal grandfather, I was able to live in Vienna and study for two years at the fashionable Theresianum academy. I would visit my love every weekend, and her family was more than kind to me. They would take me to the opera, the theater, and to shoots. For a short time, life seemed to be everything that it could ever be. Annelie was seven years older than I, but I never even thought about it. Thanks to her, I studied very hard. It was not easy to switch from Hungarian to German, when translating from Latin, and to study mathematics and politics at the same time. I nonetheless graduated in June 1938.

By then, Hitler had occupied Austria, and I remember standing in a vast crowd with Annelie's family and watching the Führer's triumphal entry into Vienna. The Austrians gave him a tumultuous welcome, with Nazi flags flying from hundreds of windows. Everyone was talking about war, and we were convinced that Hitler would conquer whatever the other powers allowed him to seize.

In September, I enrolled at the Royal University of Saint Elizabeth, at Pécs, in southern Hungary. I had decided to become a career diplomat and would be required to obtain a doctorate in political science before joining the Foreign Office. However, I had also reached the age when military service was traditional in our family. Every able-bodied nobleman was expected to serve in the army for one or two years. If he was not accepted, it was embarrassing – definitely not "ewe". Knowing this, the university excused me from attending classes and permitted me to study on my own. But with Europe sliding into war, my studies would be repeatedly interrupted.

On March 1, 1939, when I was eighteen, I volunteered for the cavalry, and my request to join the 3rd or "Nádasdy" Hussars was granted. Organized in 1683, this regiment was the oldest in the Hungarian army. It was also the best. My brother, Paul, had already served in the same unit, and through him I had come to

As a lieutenant, during World War II

know a number of the officers. The regiment had been stationed at Sopron, near the Austrian frontier, and I had gone there with Annelie on weekends for fox and drag hunts, when I was studying in Vienna. Moreover, our relative, Major General Baron Ferenc Stephaich de Nemes-Déd, whom I've already mentioned, had commanded this regiment from 1797 to 1801. During my own years of service, our colonel was Baron Pál Pongrácz, who proved to be a capable and highly respected commander.

As I am one of the last surviving cavalry officers and a veteran of the most destructive war that has ever been fought, let me tell you about our elite cavalry division and its component hussar regiments.

In war and peace, ours was the force that carried on Hungary's ancient and honored tradition of military horsemanship. The first Hungarians, who came from the Don River basin in the steppes of central Asia, were already accomplished horsemen when they occupied present-day Hungary in the ninth century. They rode small sturdy horses, like the ones that had carried Genghis Khan's armies from Mongolia all the way to Vienna. Little wonder that in Hungary the horse has always been a precious, dearly-beloved creature.

"Huzár" is a Hungarian word. "Huz" means "20", and "ár" was a unit of money in the eighteenth century. (How this relates to a cavalryman I don't pretend to know.)

A hussar regiment numbered about 510 officers and men – two battalions, each with three 85-man companies.

The 1st Hussars always remained in Hungary to train men and horses for the other regiments. In wartime, the other regiments would do the fighting, and the 1st would replace their losses.

Our Elite Cavalry Division, also had two battalions of horse artillery, one battalion of motorized field guns, a battalion of engineers and sappers, a squadron of motorcycle troops, and even a battalion of bicycle troops. The records indicate that at one point during my service the division had 517 officers, 14,257 enlisted men, 10,655 horses (of which we lost over 7,000 in World War II), 830 trucks and automobiles, 11,082 carbines, 1,867 machine pistols, 326 motorcycles, and 500 bicycles.

To become an officer in a hussar regiment you had to come from a family whose nobility was officially recognized before 1848. You had to be a high school graduate and at least eighteen years of age. You had to disclose your academic record, your religion, and submit a thumbnail genealogy. You also had to list your family's assets. Teenagers with empty pockets were under no pressure to apply. A volunteer in the Hungarian armed forces could choose the service he wanted to enter – cavalry, infantry, artillery, or air force.

In the hussar regiments, we had active officers and reserve officers. An active officer was a professional soldier, a careerist in the army. He would have to train at a military academy for four years and would graduate as a lieutenant. He would remain in the army until retirement, for active military service was a profession, like medicine or the law. By contrast, a reserve officer would be trained to the level of command and would then be provisionally discharged, but he could be called back into service on short notice, if there were a national emergency.

In peacetime, as a hussar officer, you would be stationed in a country village, on account of the horses. Your daily routine would consist of training, drilling, and studying. In your spare time, you could watch or take part in a variety of equestrian events: point-to-point races, show jumping, and fox hunts. There was lively competition for the prizes that were awarded on these occasions. On weekends, there would be bird shooting. You could also read or just drink, smoke, and play cards.

There would be dinners and balls in the evenings – the local girls and their families made sure of that. On these occasions, you wore a gala dress uniform, with large Brandenburg links on your chest and spurs on your boots. The girls would be impressed by your uniform. Hussar officers were always welcome in the best families.

Among the active (professional) officers, there was lively competition for the top commands. Once you were a colonel, you would want to command a regiment. Or, if you were multilingual, you might become a military attaché at one of the foreign legations. Otherwise, you might want to join the prestigious Ministry of War.

When I put on my uniform as a Nádasdy Hussar in March 1939, the regiment was stationed at Munkács, a garrison town in what was then northeastern Hungary. Our base was quite extensive. We had a large barracks and stable space for a thousand horses, as well as a riding academy with an indoor ring. Every barracks would house about 60 hussars, and a stable, about 60 horses.

Basic training took three months, and it was tough. I had a stripe on my sleeve to signal that I was a volunteer and was qualified to become an officer. But that made no difference because I wasn't an officer *yet*, and during basic training, I was treated just like a common soldier.

In summer, the day began at 5:00 A.M., in winter at 6:00. After breakfast, which was coffee and a piece of bread, we would head for the stables, feed and water the horses, and brush them until they really shone. By 9:00 A.M., we would be training on horseback.

Coming from my background, I was already a capable rider and could go through the equestrian exercises without much difficulty. But the inexperienced riders had a rough time. They were repeatedly thrown off, and the clumsiest ones were almost as often on the ground as in the saddle. At 11 A.M., we would ride back to the stables and brush our horses with fistfuls of straw in both hands.

At lunch time, a horrible goulash would be ladled out to us. At 2:00 P.M. would come the drill. A military band would begin to play, and we would march to martial music and sing to help us stay in time. On special occasions, we would march to the music of a mounted regimental band, and the horses would be all of the same color. These musical equestrian drills were spectacular and were always well attended.

I recall that in the German-Polish War of 1939 we welcomed two fugitive Polish cavalry regiments that were still perfectly uniformed and with their mounted bands playing. We greeted them as friends and put them up in our barracks. Our willingness to intern these refugees in Hungary may have saved their officers from falling into Soviet hands and being murdered in Katyn Forest.

During basic training, we were not permitted to leave the base, and at 8:00 P.M., it was "lights out" in the barracks. After the first three months, we could go to Munkács, and it was a pleasure to walk to town in uniform with perfectly polished boots and to have a hot chocolate with whipped cream. But we were still not permitted to mingle with the townspeople. More than half of them were Orthodox Jews, and if the truth must be told, their standards of hygiene were deplorable.

Eventually, the volunteers – about fifty of us – were transferred to a town with an unpronounceable name. There, at the training school for hussar officers, we found ourselves in more agreeable circumstances. We would have two hours of lessons and a great deal of riding. We were now permitted to bring in our own horses, but we still had to care for them ourselves. My mount was a bay which I had obtained from the Apponyi family. Its name was Hiuz, which means "lynx".

Our riding exercises were recklessly challenging. We had to gallop over high jumps without saddle or bridle and urge our horses down almost perpendicular earthen embankments. Once

Hussars training

Hussars training

a week, we performed an exercise called *voltiger*. The horse would canter in a circle on a long rope, and the hussar would have to stand up on its back and then sit down again and do a number of other stunts. Worst of all, as we were performing these dangerous exercises, the sergeant would be trying his damndest to make us fall off.

Virginity was not tolerated among the hussars. One day, while we were sitting on our benches studying, the sergeant loudly demanded, "Is there anyone here who has never slept with a woman? If so, STAND UP!" A stupid friend of mine started to get up. I grabbed him and tried to pull him back down, but it was too late. The poor fellow was marched to the nearest bordello and forced to make love, with the sergeant looking on. When he came back, he was a certified non-virgin. But his love life got off to a rocky start. Within two weeks, he was in the hospital with gonorrhea.

After five months, we were transferred back to Munkács, our initial base, but we were now sergeants, and our circumstances had again improved. We were allowed to live off base and could keep apartments in town, but by 5:00 or 6:00 A.M. we would have to report for duty.

I was now given command of ten hussars – a platoon. I would buy extra shoe polish and brushes so that my men would look better than the rest. And we officers were now permitted to order custom-made uniforms from a tailor who would come from Budapest.

But there was still a problem: While we were not permitted to mingle with the townspeople, we were also reluctant to socialize with our married superior officers, because their wives had a way of making passes at well-groomed, good-looking young sergeants.

So what did we do? In our region, the bordellos were all controlled by the state, like little clubs. Each one had a good restaurant, Gypsy music, and a relaxing atmosphere. If a button was missing on your uniform, "les girls" would sew it on. And if you wanted more than a button sewed on, there was a delightful choice. Afterwards, the girl would give you a shower and a massage, polish your boots – whatever you wanted. On the outer door of our favorite establishment was a sign that read, "Everything". We were all friends, and there was plenty of laughter. It was such a joy to be nineteen.

When off duty, we officers would read, smoke and chat, drink and play cards. There was an officers' mess, or club, but we didn't like to go there because often there would be an incident and someone would get in trouble. So, with three other officers, two of them from my beloved county of Somogy, I transformed a little Jewish shop near our barracks into a private club for the four of us.

But I'm getting ahead of myself. It was in March 1939, just a few days after my enlistment, that I was shot at for the first time (but not the last!).

Hitler was chopping off pieces of Czechoslovakia, which he had overrun the previous year, and hoping to keep a neighbor country friendly, he restored Ruthenia to Hungary. This province had belonged to our country for many centuries but had been awarded to Czechoslovakia in 1920 by the vengeful Treaty of Trianon.

Our base at Munkács was right next to Ruthenia, and one day, while I was on duty at the frontier, I struck up a conversation with the friendly Czech border guard standing just across from me. He persuaded me to come over to his side of the barrier, and we smoked and chatted for a while. It was all very friendly. But the next day, the same guard saw me approaching the border and promptly took a shot at me with his rifle.

"WHAT ARE YOU DOING???" I screamed. "It's ME!" He then shot at me again and immediately ran away. That was how I learned that Ruthenia had been formally returned to Hungary. However, the local people remained friendly when we marched in to repossess the lost province, because they were all Hungarians.

Those who have read *Mein Kampf* will understand that Hitler's final objective was to conquer the cradle of communism, Soviet Russia, and to overthrow its mighty dictator, Joseph Stalin. The resulting clash, World War II, was the most frightful disaster since the Great Plague of 1348. A grand total of fifty million people were killed. Hitler murdered almost six million civilians. Stalin killed many more with his paranoid purges, Arctic concentration camps, genocidal suppression of minorities, agricultural catastrophes, and forcible relocations of uprooted nationalities. But his specialty was to kill people's hearts and minds. Hitler's Reich disappeared with his death, but Stalin built a sinister empire in Eastern and Central Europe that outlived him and reduced more than a hundred million people to slavery for over forty years. He killed or drove out anyone who rejected the monolithic form of communism known as Stalinism. That is how I came to lose my home, my possessions, and worst of all my beloved country, and was forced to live like an immigrant and refugee for the rest of my life.

In 1939, poor Poland was caught between the German and Soviet dictators. Hitler did not want to wage war on two fronts, so he concluded a cynical non-aggression pact with Stalin, which provided for Poland to be divided. When Germany invaded, the Poles fought heroically, especially their cavalry, but they were defeated in three weeks. Britain and France had guaranteed Poland's sovereignty, and they declared war on Germany, but not on Soviet Russia. They also sent no military assistance to Poland.

In the summer of 1940, we were again mobilized. Hitler was now chopping off pieces of Romania and giving them back to their former owners. Having made an uneasy peace with Stalin, the Nazi dictator allowed Soviet troops to seize Bessarabia. By the Second Vienna Award, he forced Romania to cede Dobruja to Bulgaria and to return Transylvania to Hungary, which had previously owned it for a thousand years.

Hitler took our Regent, Admiral Horthy, for a ride.

The reserve officers were called up, my brother Paul among them, and the Nádasdy Hussars marched into Transylvania. But war did not break out, because Britain and France chose not to oppose Hitler's division of Romania. We found ourselves in a lovely mountainous region of pine forests and trout streams. Our regiment was greeted warmly, for the people were ethnic Hungarians. I found the girls good-looking – and very cooperative.

Before long, we returned to Munkács, the reserve officers went home, and the daily grind of training, drilling, and studying resumed.

By then, Hitler had conquered France in a five-week *blitzkrieg* that amazed and alarmed the world. As Nazi Germany grew steadily bolder and continued to succeed in its aggressions, our Regent, Admiral Horthy, decided that an alliance with Hitler might enable us to regain all of the territories we had lost by the Treaty of Trianon. At the same time, he was privately convinced that Germany would eventually lose the war. His decision, in November 1940, to lead Hungary into the Rome-Tokyo-Berlin Axis was therefore a complicated and dangerous gamble. With Hitler's assistance, Horthy might possibly repossess all of the lost Hungarian territories. What remained to be seen was whether he could disengage from the Nazi dictator before Germany was defeated. For the time being, Horthy was "in bed" with Hitler. He had made a deal with the devil.

In April 1941, we were mobilized again, this time against Yugoslavia. The Greek army had thrown back Mussolini's laughable invasion, and Hitler was now required to send eighteen German divisions through Hungary and Yugoslavia to defeat the Greeks. In Belgrade, the British ambassador persuaded the teenaged monarch, King Peter II, to seize power from his Regent, Prince Paul, and to appoint an anti-German government. Hitler reacted by invading Yugoslavia, and some Hungarian troops, including our cavalry division, reoccupied a portion of Croatia which had been torn from Hungary and awarded to Yugoslavia by the Allied Powers, in 1920.

We advanced down the Danube to about 80 kilometers northwest of Belgrade. There we had to halt because the Regent Horthy had ordered us not to advance beyond the limits of pre-Trianon Hungary. At Novi Sad, we took up defensive positions, because the Yugoslav army was directly in front of us. There were several skirmishes. The Serbian troops fought bravely, and about fifteen of us were killed, including one of my friends. But the German troops conquered Yugoslavia, on their way to Greece, and we were soon ordered back to Hungary. We had been ordered to reoccupy the region of Croatia that had been Hungarian, and we had accomplished that. The campaign also gave us some excitement, and I recall that we had lots of fun with the reserve officers who had been called back into service.

Hitler had wanted to invade the Soviet Union in April 1941 under the plan known as Operation Barbarossa, but he was forced to postpone his attack until Greece and Yugoslavia were defeated. Finally, on June 22nd, he launched the historic invasion, but by then it was way overdue, and he would miss the 18 divisions he had sent to prop up Mussolini. This contributed to Hitler's first defeat, at Christmas, when the *blitzkrieg* stalled before Moscow.

Hungary did not participate in the initial invasion of Russia. The Regent Horthy was determined to keep us out of that misadventure. But Hitler's leverage over him prevailed, and all too soon Hungary was forced to send troops to the Soviet front.

After our thrust into Yugoslavia, we were sent back to the officers' training school, where we had become volunteer sergeants. Old friendships were renewed. As always, we exercised our horses in the mornings, but now we had grooms to take care of them. Our afternoons were taken up with classes that lasted from 2:00 until 6:00 P.M.

I remember an incident that took place at the officers' training school. A cousin of mine, Count Balázs Forgach, invited me to shoot partridges, and I arranged for my friend Peter Urban to join us. Peter was a nephew of the Regent Horthy's wife. More important, he had a car, and we needed one.

Because a military uniform is uncomfortable when shooting partridges, we decided to wear civilian clothes. While having breakfast at a café, we spotted a colonel from the General Staff at another table. We tried to disappear, but it was too late. He called us back and reminded us, "You are not allowed to wear civilian clothes, and you know it. Report to your commanding officer immediately!" We were sentenced to ten days of imprisonment in a filthy room. Those were the ten longest days of my life.

Here are some particulars about our dress code. Ordinarily, we wore what was known as "small gala" – a well-cut khaki jacket, black trousers, low boots that reached to the middle foreleg, spurs, a broad shiny leather belt, and a black kepi hat that we never took off, not to salute or even in the presence of ladies.

A hussar officer had to carry arms at all times – a pistol in a shiny leather holster or a sword. Even in a restaurant he had to be armed in order to defend his honor if someone attacked him. The swords of active (professional) officers were occasionally quite beautiful. Some had been passed from father to son for generations.

Like all noble Hungarians, hussars were intensely preoccupied with their honor and frequently challenged each other to duels. If a drunken officer shouted that your lady friend was a tramp, that your colonel was a thief, and that His Serene Highness The Regent Horthy was nothing but a damn fool, you would either throw a glove in his face or coldly hand him your greeting card. You would then report the incident to the regimental dueling committee, which would decide the particulars of the duel – whether swords or pistols would be used and whether you would fight to first blood or to final exhaustion. In old Hungary, a surprising number of people were killed in duels. Military officers were prohibited from dueling only during mobilization. I was never involved in a duel myself, but every Hungarian nobleman was taught how to behave if mortally insulted.

In Hungary, the cavalry included all the mounted troops – dragoons, uhlans, and hussars. The hussars were the light cavalry. The well-bred Hungarian horses that carried these troopers were among the finest in the world. Consider what one of them had to carry: first the rider, then the saddle, then the rider's food and gear, then the weapons (carbine, pistol, and sword), then the ammunition, and finally the horse's fodder – in all, about 140 kilos. I well remember that our longest march, without stopping to feed or water the horses and pausing only to adjust the saddles, covered 90 kilometers and lasted 11 hours. When a cavalry unit was in transit, the horses were never cantered. The troopers would walk or trot their mounts in two columns on opposite sides of the road. The bugler, who was always beside the commanding officer, would signal for us to walk or trot. He would also bugle for us to rise in the morning and to retire at night. His was an important role.

The national flag of Hungary, which features a crown of Saint Stephen on bars of red, green, and white, flew over all of our bases and encampments, and it had to be saluted, always, by everyone.

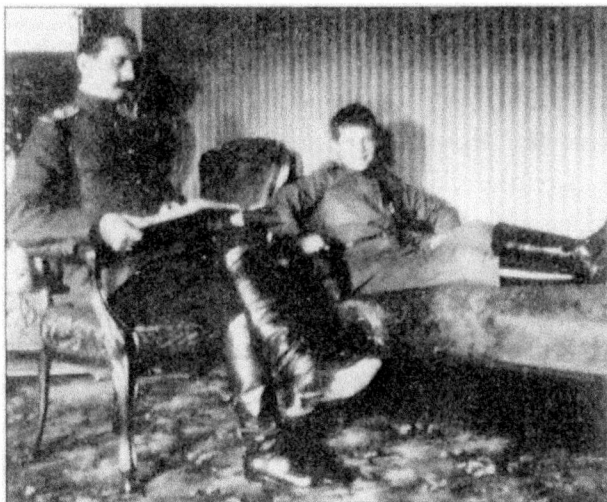
My French teacher, Pierre Gilliard, with his better-known pupil, Czarevitch Alexis

Our regimental colors were also green and red but featured a hand-sewn silken likeness of Saint Mary, patroness of Hungary.

As hussars, we were taught to fight with swords. A straw dummy would be placed in standing position, and we would have to slash it while passing at a gallop. During my several military campaigns, every hussar carried a sword, but no one had to use one, except to salute.

In 1942, there was a short period of comparative peace. I was a second lieutenant in the reserves by then, and I asked Colonel Pongrácz for a leave of absence to study at Lausanne, Switzerland. Fluency in French was required for a career in the Foreign Office, and I wanted to improve my command of that language.

"You want to eat chocolate in Switzerland when all of Europe is in flames!" my colonel jested.

"I give you my word of honor that I'll return if you send for me," I shot back. "If you doubt my word, I will have to challenge you to a duel, being an officer myself." Laughing, he agreed, and I studied at the University of Lausanne for several months. My

French teacher was Pierre Gilliard, who had tutored Czarevitch Alexis, the son of Czar Nicholas II. Gilliard had survived the massacre of the Russian imperial family and had returned to Lausanne, after a complicated and romantic escape, but unfortunately he seldom related his adventures.

At Lausanne, I had a wonderful time with the numerous French, Polish, and Spanish refugees. We formed a soccer team which included Don Juan, Count of Barcelona, then pretender to the Spanish throne, his brother, Don Jaime, who was deaf and dumb but could still play soccer, Fernando de la Cerda, and three members of the Italian Stagni family, who were refugees from Egypt and lived in the Palace Hotel. When we needed extra players, the Stagnis would phone the hotel manager and ask him to send over some employees who could play the game.

I remember having tea with Queen Victoria Eugenia of Spain, the widow of King Alfonso XIII, who lived with her family in a small hotel at Lausanne. The whole Spanish royal family were charming – very simple, wonderful company and very popular.

All the while, I had been corresponding with Annelie, who now informed me that she had to return to Vienna because her family was having problems with the Nazis.

At last, after six months, Colonel Pongrácz telegraphed me to come back, ending my Swiss sojourn. I returned to the Hussars and was happy to see old friends. But it was then that I received a letter from Annelie telling me that, for security reasons, she had decided to marry an Italian diplomat, a great friend of hers, who later became the consul general in Córdoba, Argentina. The three of us remained friends, but Annelie died of cancer at an early age. My brother is the godfather of her eldest daughter.

During all these years, I had studied alone for my graduation from the university at Pécs whenever time permitted, but I had not attended any classes. My oral exam was now scheduled for January 17, 1943. To prepare myself, I obtained a two weeks' leave of absence from the Hussars and studied twelve to fourteen hours daily at a nearby school. I also had a tutor.

At last, my day of reckoning arrived. The civilian candidates for diplomas appeared in cutaways or in Hungarian gala. Being an officer, I wore my dress uniform with decorations. Five professors, one after another, put questions to me for four or five hours.

When the rector of the university remarked, "We have not had the pleasure of meeting you before, Mr. Stephaich!" I explained how I had been exempted from attending classes because of my military service. Later that day, after consulting with the other four professors, the rector congratulated me for being so well prepared. My doctoral thesis had already been sent to them.

So I received the doctorate in political science, which qualified me for a Foreign Office career. The actual diploma, which no one has ever looked at, hangs in my bathroom over the toilet. My brother, Paul, had been in the Foreign Office for the previous four years, and through him I came to know many of the important big-wigs.

I passed the first exam for the Foreign Office easily. The Ministry advised my regiment that the second and final exam would come at the end of a one-year course, so I was not obliged to return to the Hussars for the time being.

There were seven candidates for the final exam. Each of us had to give a detailed curriculum vitae, a résumé of his family background, and a disclosure of his financial situation. Our salaries were so low that no one could have lived on them, so we needed extra cash from our own pockets. Similarly, when a Foreign Office official wanted to get married, he had to disclose his fiancée's social background and his own income. This careful screening, which each of us had to undergo when applying for the Foreign Office or a cavalry regiment, caused us to feel like one big family.

In February 1944, when I had passed the second exam, a letter arrived from Foreign Minister Jénö Ghyczy, countersigned by Prime Minister Miklós de Kállay, confirming that I had been appointed third secretary of the Foreign Office for six months, but with no salary. I was immediately assigned to the counter-espionage and passport departments. It was dull administrative work.

I got to know my colleagues and was introduced to the minister and the heads of the Political, Economic, and Protocol departments. Most of them knew my name and welcomed me with open arms. That we were all anti-fascist and also anti-communist helped us to become friends. But we were deceiving ourselves when we believed that it would be possible for a small country, so close to the two totalitarian giants and so far from the Western Allies, to avoid being occupied by either Nazi Germany or the Soviet Union. As it turned out, we would be occupied by both.

The German Occupation,
The Mass Murder of Hungarian Jews,
The War with Russia, the Destruction of Warsaw

In March 1944, Hitler summoned the Regent of Hungary, Admiral Miklós Horthy, to an urgent private meeting at Klessheim Castle, near Salzburg. With enormous Soviet armies approaching our eastern frontier, the Nazi dictator informed Horthy that for defensive purposes he had been forced to order the immediate occupation of Hungary by 60,000 German troops. Shouting and pounding the table, he reminded the Regent that Hungary's alliance with Germany was the only hope of avoiding a Soviet invasion followed by enforced communization.

The Regent of Hungary, Admiral Miklós Horthy (1868-1957),
our acting chief-of-state and commander-in-chief

The Führer's words must have caused Horthy to reflect bitterly
on the irony of his predicament. He had befriended Hitler hoping
that with German diplomatic and military support Hungary
could repossess her lost provinces. And now Horthy found
himslef linked to Hitler like a Siamese twin, because Hitler was
all that stood between him and Stalin.

The Führer then presented Horthy with a brutal choice: He could remain in power if he authorized the presence of German troops on Hungarian soil. If he refused, the German occupation would proceed anyway, the Regency would be abolished, and Hungary would become a Nazi colony governed directly from Berlin.

Painfully, Horthy decided that continued collaboration would be the lesser evil, so he agreed to Hitler's outrageous demand. This left him free to act within a shrinking political sphere, but from that day on he could make no important decision without carefully weighing how the Führer would react. To underscore the new balance of power, Hitler stationed his personal plenipotentiary, SS Oberführer Dr. Edmund Veesenmayer, in Budapest with orders to keep Horthy under surveillance and to communicate the Führer's wishes to him.

On March 18th, I got a phone call from the girlfriend of a well-placed SS officer, informing me that German troops would occupy our country on the following day. I immediately called my brother, Paul, at the Hungarian Consulate in Vienna and asked him, in our code language, what he knew. He confirmed that many "friends" were about to descend on Hungary.

My first obligation was to warn the people we knew who had reason to fear a German occupation. Among these were the Ullmanns. Gyuri was my best friend, his sister, Erzsébet, a lovely sweetheart, and their father was the president of a bank in which the Austrian Rothschilds held a one-quarter interest.

On March 19th, Erzsébet phoned me to say that "friends" had indeed arrived at her father's bank and were on their way to her home. I threw on my uniform and rushed to the Ullmanns' on my motorbike. The family was panic-stricken and the house crammed with excited refugees. We sent the father of Erzsébet and Gyuri to hide in a tiny apartment above the shop of his barber; he lived there in terror for many months without once coming down to the street. Erzsébet was sent to some friends named Satzger, who lived in the country, and I arranged for my father's friend, General Béla Lengyel, to induct Gyuri into the Hungarian army, gambling that our Nazi invaders would not look for him there. I was the only one whom the Germans took away for questioning, and they grilled me for three or four hours. Once released, I went to the Foreign Office and told my colleagues what had happened. They informed me that three of our leading diplomats had already been arrested.

Because the cold-blooded murder of our large Jewish minority was one of the most horrifying crimes in recent history, I cannot pass over it in silence. The religious difference between Jews and Christians is unfortunately fundamental: Christians believe in Christ, Jews do not. Anti-Semitism has therefore occurred in every country where both Jews and Christians are found. Undeniably, it was still a social and political fact-of-life in Hungary during the 1930s and '40s, but no more so than in Poland, Romania, Bulgaria, Croatia, or the Baltic States.

At the beginning of 1944, the population of Hungary, including the regions we had repossessed with German backing, totaled about 15 million, of which roughly 825,000 were Jews. In the space of a single year, more than 65 percent of our Jewish population would be murdered by the Germans and their collaborators, the Hungarian fascists.

When Nazi Germany became the driving force behind European anti-Semitism, Hungary found itself in an extremely difficult position. Economically, we had been heavily dependent on Germany for many years. Even before Hitler came to power, our armed forces were equipped with German weapons and military hardware, and in 1938 our principal trading partner, Austria, was forced into union with Nazi Germany. But most important of all, our desperate efforts to regain, with German assistance, the regions of Hungary that were still under Czech, Romanian, and

Yugoslav occupation gave Hitler tremendous leverage over our internal and foreign affairs. He used this leverage to maneuver us into his military alliance, the Axis, and to make us adopt anti-Jewish legislation similar to that of Nazi Germany.

To placate Hitler, the Regent Horthy had appointed two anti-Semitic prime ministers, Béla Imrédy (1938-39) and László Bárdossy (1941-42). These leaders had enacted laws that stripped Jews of the full civil rights which they had enjoyed in Hungary since 1867. They were excluded from the military and civil services and from key professions. They were also prohibited from marrying gentiles, though almost no Jew wanted to do so. I nonetheless insist that our government would never have enacted anti-Jewish laws, much less collaborated in the massacre of our Jewish minority, had it not been for intense and persistent pressure from Nazi Germany.

Privately, Horthy had always doubted that Hitler could win the war, and Prime Minister Miklós de Kállay (1942-44) shared his doubts. But as long as Hitler appeared to be keeping Stalin at bay, Horthy and Kállay were willing to go along for the ride. What compelled them to reconsider their collaboration was the catastrophic defeat of the German and Hungarian armies at Stalingrad, in early 1943. Left with little hope for an Axis victory, Horthy and Kállay began to angle for an armistice with the Allies, but their secret informal diplomatic contacts were quickly discovered by the Germans. Hitler occupied Hungary in March 1944 to prevent its defection from the Axis and to protect his supply lines to the Eastern Front. But he was also eager to impose his "Final Solution" on a country where, in his view, the "Jewish Problem" had not yet been "solved."

To his credit, Horthy had always dragged his feet when Hitler prodded him to impose the full Holocaust on our numerous Jewish minority. But his tactful evasiveness became increasingly difficult after Germany invaded and occupied us. In March 1944, the Führer cast diplomacy aside and demanded that Horthy remove Prime Minister Kállay from office and reappoint the anti-Semite, Imrédy, to head our government. With deep regret, the Regent dismissed Kállay, but he refused to reappoint Imrédy and proposed that the Führer accept our right-wing general, Döme Sztójay, instead. General Sztójay had been the Hungarian minister to Germany for many years, and since he was friendly with the Nazi leaders, Hitler agreed to his appointment.

Admiral Horthy and General Sztójay were military men of the highest rank, and Horthy would later claim that, as commander-in-chief, he had believed he could count on Sztójay's personal loyalty. He would also claim to have regarded the general as a patriot who could be relied on to place Hungary's interests above Hitler's demands. If Horthy really believed all that, he misjudged Sztójay completely, for the new prime minister immediately appointed a number of leading Nazi sympathizers and anti-Semites to his cabinet.

The moment Hitler occupied Hungary, the Germans began to arrest and detain important Jewish individuals like my friends the Ullmanns. In April, they embarked on a massive program to intern and deport our entire Jewish population. The Jews of Budapest were spared for a few more months, but those who lived in the rest of Hungary were swiftly shunted off to the giant Nazi death factory know as Auschwitz, in German-occupied Poland. It is shameful that the Sztójay government ordered hundreds of Hungarian police officers to collaborate with the Germans in this brazenly undisguised genocide. Our government also legalized the anti-Semitic Hungarian fascist party known as the Arrow Cross and legitimized its leader, Ferenc Szálasi.

That Germany's "Final Solution" was being imposed on Hungarian Jews by Hitler and Sztójay soon placed the Regent Horthy in serious danger. On "D Day", an overwhelming number of Allied troops stormed ashore in Normandy, opening a third front in the war and virtually guaranteeing Germany's defeat. That Prime Minister Churchill and President Roosevelt were threatening to try the Axis leaders for crimes against humanity can only have sent a chill through Horthy. On July 6th, when it was far too late, he issued an order halting the deportation of all Hungarian subjects, including Jews, but the Germans paid no attention to the order, and with Hitler's iron backing our prime minister disregarded it too. When the Regent threatened to remove Sztójay from office, Hitler overruled him.

Before many months had gone by, more than half a million Hungarian Jews had been murdered. Most of them perished in the gas chambers of Auschwitz, but countless others were shot, beaten, starved, or worked to death in forced labor gangs on the Eastern Front.

The primary responsibility for this atrocity rests on Hitler, for he was the driving force behind it. But the willing collaboration of the Sztójay government, was scarcely less reprehensible. And while the International Military Tribunal at Nürnberg would fail to charge the Regent Horthy with complicity in genocide, one has to wonder why he hesitated for three fatal months before making any appreciable effort to halt the bloodbath.

When the war ended, Dóme Sztójay was sentenced to death for genocide and shot by a Hungarian firing squad. Prime ministers Imrédy and Bárdossy were also executed, as were several members of General Sztójay's cabinet.

In fact, between 1918 and 1946, four Hungarian prime ministers were shot, one was hanged, one died in jail, two were driven out by the Germans, and one committed suicide. Several others resigned in despair or were fired by Horthy. To be a Hungarian prime minister has not always been a bed of roses.

In the spring of 1944, just as the Holocaust was being imposed in Hungary, Hitler pressured our government to increase the number of Hungarian troops on the Eastern Front. It was then

General Mihály de Ibrányi, who commanded the Elite Cavelry Division, in which I served

that I received a telegram ordering me to rejoin the Hussars immediately. The Elite Cavalry Division, which included our regiment, was to depart for the Soviet Union with all possible haste. We were marshaled at Nagyvárad, in Transylvania, and proceeded to the front by rail. Because I was fluent in German, I was assigned to the staff as aide-de-camp to our divisional commander, General Mihály de Ibrányi. This proved to be an interesting and important position for a young man.

It may seem curious that cavalry was still useful in combat as late as 1944, but there were sound reasons for this. Vast areas of Russia were covered with dense forest where tanks could not penetrate but horsemen could move easily and swiftly. Also, the Russian winters were so cold that the engine oil in the tanks and other military vehicles would occasionally freeze and make them useless.

We had a German liaison group with us – a colonel, a captain, and a lieutenant – with all the necessary radio and other equipment. They were cavalry officers and gentlemen. I became a close friend of Captain Gerhard Bolt, who had already been wounded eight times. His specialty was to destroy Soviet tanks with explosives. He would run up and jump onto the tank, open the turret, throw in the explosive, jump off again, and then, if any soldiers crawled out of the burning wreckage, he would finish them off with his machine pistol. Bolt was appropriately decorated and survived the war.

At one point, we were fighting between Pinsk and Lunin, on the southern edge of the Pripet Marshes. This region is in Byelorussia, just north of the Ukraine. To the north lay thousands of square miles of swamp where the Soviet partisans would hide, sometimes underwater while breathing through rubber tubes or steel rods. Here and there, the Germans had laid down wooden planking to make "roads" through the marshes. As we passed, the partisans would rise out of the water and shoot at us from behind, often with devastating effect. We lost a very fine general there.

That summer, Marshal Konstantin Rokossovsky hurled 160,000 Soviet troops against our sector of the front. Needless to say, in numbers, weapons, and experience, we were not equal to these veterans of Stalingrad. On July 4, 1944, our division lost sixty percent of its officers and forty-five percent of its men. All six officers of the squadron in which I had previously served were killed or unaccounted for. Every one of them was a close friend of mine.

Let me tell you about an experience I had during those terrible weeks.

An entire battalion of Hungarian troops had disappeared without a trace, and General Ibrányi ordered me to search for it. My first problem was to determine the whereabouts of the enemy. That was difficult, because in the Pripet Marshes the Russian strategy was to attack us at one point, then slip away and attack somewhere else on the following day.

One source of information was a German colonel, Freiherr von Böselager, who had arrived at our headquarters. Since he had just been wounded in heavy fighting, I asked him to tell me precisely where the front was. He replied, "Wherever the Russians are shooting at you." With these useful directions, I set out.

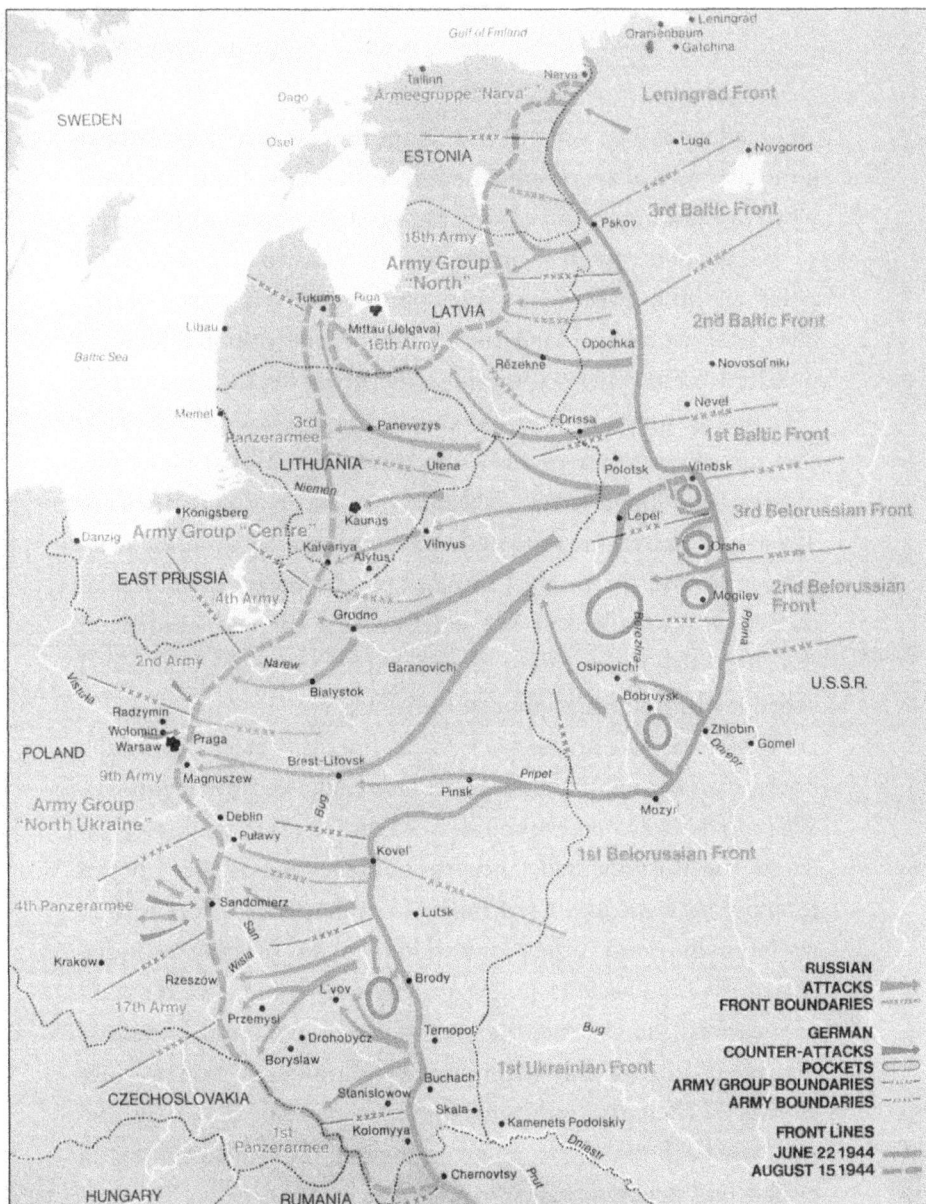

The Eastern Front, June 22nd to August 15th, 1944

My German friend, Captain Bolt, was at my side as we drove off in General Ibrányi's six-wheeled armored vehicle. A number of shoulder-held anti-tank guns – the Americans called them "bazookas" – had finally been issued to us, and I was under orders not to lose even one of them to the enemy. Luckily, we had an excellent driver, a sergeant, and another chap with a machine gun. We were also accompanied by a journalist from Budapest who was looking for adventure. He would find it soon enough.

We headed east in a desperate search for the lost battalion. After an hour's drive, we saw some soldiers in green shirts, like those worn by Hungarian troops in the summer, about a hundred meters away. Ordering our driver to stop, I shouted, "We're searching for a lost battalion." The soldiers did not react; they simply watched us. So I screamed, "You idiots! Don't you understand Hungarian???" It turned out that they were Russians. They disappeared into the high grass and started to shoot at us. We had found the front! I shouted for the driver to get out of there, but Captain Bolt jumped from the car and headed off through thick cover, intent on picking off a few of the enemy. I yelled for him to return, but he didn't answer.

When we had driven back for a short distance, I spotted a Hungarian field gun manned by a lieutenant and three gunners. We pulled it to where we could shoot directly into the high grass where the Russians had taken cover, then opened fire. I began to crawl forward like a red Indian in a desperate effort to find my German friend. When I found him, he was severely wounded and nearly unconscious. I blew into his mouth and started to pull him toward the car, but the grass was too high, and I couldn't manage it. I finally threw him over my shoulder and carried him to safety. I then gave orders for the field gun to be blown up, and we drove back to the west as fast as possible. Twelve machine-gun bullets had struck the car.

Unfortunately, we never found the lost battalion. Years later, a few of its officers trickled back from Soviet concentration camps.

The Germans wanted to give me a decoration for saving Captain Bolt, but fortunately I declined. After the war, every

Hungarian who had been decorated by the Germans had problems with the communist police.

As a member of General Ibrányi's staff, I would meet the leading German commanders when they came to our headquarters. One was Field Marshal Walther Model, who ranked high among Hitler's favorites. As commander of the 9th German Army, he had advanced to a point quite close to Moscow during the initial German invasion. In 1944, he commanded Army Group North, which included our cavalry division and all of the Axis forces in northern Russia and Poland. Always accompanied by important military brass, Field Marshal Model would arrive in his Storch aircraft to inspect our troops and to coordinate strategy with General Ibrányi. I remember that this celebrated commander of mobile mechanized units was curious and somewhat bewildered to meet a general whose division was still fighting with horses. When the war ended, Model had a choice: He could commit suicide or surrender to the Americans. He blew his brains out.

When we were fighting in Byelorussia and later in Poland, the Germans would assign us a 5-kilometer-wide sector of the front. There would be German troops on our right and left and often also behind us. But because we were fighting on enemy territory, the Russians always knew our positions, and they normally preferred to attack us, rather than the battle-hardened and better-equipped German shock troops. If the Russians broke through in our sector, General Ibrányi would order us to fall back for a few kilometers so that the Germans could counterattack.

Our communications were normally quite good. General Ibrányi kept in contact with his regimental commanders by radio telephone, and they would keep in contact with their units the same way. In an emergency, motorcyclists could be sent to carry messages, or hussars could deliver them on horseback. As a rule, our well-equipped German liaison officers were very effective at coordinating the tactical movements of their army with ours.

Retrieving the body of a fallen hussar (right), Eastern Front, summer of 1944

But on two occasions, the Germans suddenly pulled back their front line without informing us. Before we knew it, the Russians were behind us. Our troops managed to fight their way to where they had left the horses, and, once mounted, they were able to withdraw to the positions that General Ibrányi had designated. And so it went: We would fight for two or three days, until the Russians broke through, and would then fall back as ordered.

Unfortunately, we had no armaments industry in Hungary and had to rely on the Germans for weapons, ammunition, and equipment. As I have mentioned, toward the end of the war, when it was too late, they did supply us with shoulder-held anti-tank rocket launchers that were effective. But by then, the Germans were fighting on three fronts – in France and Italy, as well as Russia – and they were under such heavy pressure that we could not count on them for supplies. They would promise us a certain number of field guns, and the weapons would arrive late, or not at all, or only half of them, or the wrong kind of gun.

All through July of '44, the German and Hungarian forces retreated westward from Byelorussia through Poland, fighting a rearguard action, until they arrived on the Vistula at the bridgehead of Warsaw. In this retreat, our officers and men were continuously killed, wounded, or unaccounted for, and we received almost no replacements. The horses suffered as much as the men. We had to shoot thousands of them to end their misery.

It is said that to conduct a prolonged orderly retreat, without it becoming a rout, is the most difficult challenge in all of warfare. Faced, as we were, with impossible odds, I am proud that our troops had the discipline and the courage to implement this strategy, though the cost to life and limb was frightful.

At the Warsaw bridgehead, we were still under German command. On our left was the crack Death's Head Division of the Waffen SS, with its Tiger tanks. On our right was the similar

5th SS Panzer or Viking Division, also composed entirely of volunteers. These troops were feared and respected. They were the toughest of the tough, and Hitler saw to it that any men or equipment that they lost in battle were immediately replaced. Sandwiched between these famous fighting units was the remainder of our shattered Elite Cavalry Division, now reduced to less than half strength.

The Viking Division was commanded by General Herbert Otto Gille. He would come to our headquarters regularly, and I would meet him there. He had style. On one occasion, I had to deliver a message to him, and he offered me a properly-chilled drink of the best champagne. General Gille was more than effective and brave. In February 1945, he was given the impossible order to liberate the German forces that were encircled by the Russians at Budapest. He made a heroic attempt to break the siege, but he arrived too late, when the Soviet troops were already far too numerous. For his outstanding courage and ability, General Gille was permitted to add oak leaves, swords, and diamonds to his Iron Cross.

But among the numerous military figures I met, Colonel Hans-Ulrich Rudel stands out from the rest. Recklessly brave, he was the most decorated German serviceman in World War II and the most famous combat flier since Baron Manfried von Richthofen. I met him after the war at a German spa, where I was taking the waters with my friends Peter Salm and Didi Kesselstatt, and we had a few whiskies together. It wasn't necessary for Rudel to tell us his story – everyone knew what he had done.

In September 1941, while flying a Stuka dive-bomber, Rudel had scored a direct hit on the Soviet battleship, Marat, and had put it on the bottom. By November 1942, he had flown 1,600 missions and had wiped out more than 100 Soviet tanks. His tactic of flying at very low altitude – sometimes just a few feet above the ground, when approaching a target – had paid off handsomely.

Field Marshal Walther Model

General Herbert Otto Gille

Colonel Hans-Ulrich Rudel

When Rudel had won every German decoration for bravery, Hitler directed the firm of Godet, in Berlin, to make an award especially for him, an Iron Cross that featured two diamond-studded 18-karat gold swords with matching oak leaves.

The sight of Rudel standing before him, with one leg missing and visible wounds in various parts of the body, softened even Hitler's stony heart, and he ordered the hero never to fly again. But when Rudel firmly refused to accept the new award unless he was allowed to return to his squadron, the Führer backed down and permitted him to keep flying.

Rudel never fought on the Western Front, only in the East against the Russians. His final score for the war was 2,530 missions, one Soviet battleship, two cruisers, one destroyer, 70 other craft sunk or wrecked, 150 artillery pieces, 4 armored trains, 800 other vehicles, and 519 enemy tanks, of which 26 were destroyed while he was flying with one leg. Rudel was never shot down by another pilot, only by enemy ground fire, but he was forced to crash-land his plane on 32 occasions and several times behind enemy lines.

Incredibly, he survived the war and then surprised everyone again by becoming a successful businessman. I'm proud to have swum in the same pool with Hans-Ulrich Rudel!

But let's return to the summer of 1944. The front was quiet for several days, after we arrived at Warsaw, but on August 1st, General Tadeusz ("Bór") Komorowski launched the memorable Polish Uprising. At 5:00 P.M., all over the city, windows flew open and hundreds of partisans started shooting at the Germans.

When General Ibrányi ordered me to find out what was happening, I made contact with two members of the Free Polish underground. We would meet anonymously at night and communicate in French. I learned that the situation in Warsaw was appalling. Wild with rage, the Germans had embarked on an orgy of murder that was bizarre even by their standards. They were going from cellar to cellar and burning the occupants alive with flame-throwers. Women, children, babies – no one was spared. Fires broke out all over the city. At the same time, the Americans were trying to bomb German targets with their "Flying Fortresses", but they would often miss by as much as a mile.

I remember spotting an American pilot who had parachuted from his burning plane. With my BMW 750 motorcycle, I eventually found him in a field and gave him a drink and some cigarettes before the Germans took him away.

By then, the Russians were marshaling their enormous army to force a passage over the Vistula and take Warsaw. Prime Minister Churchill begged Stalin to send troops into the Polish capital to help the partisans, but the Free Poles were opposed to communism, and Stalin was determined to let the Germans annihilate them before he annihilated the Germans. As it turned out, the mighty Soviet army remained safely east of the Vistula and did not move. The Germans murdered 200,000 Poles, almost all of them unarmed civilians. The brutality that I witnessed at Warsaw completely beggars the imagination, but it failed to disturb the Russians, because they knew that the Poles hated them just as much as they hated the Germans. Eventually, the entire Polish capital was destroyed – most of it by the Germans, the rest by Soviet artillery and American bombing. Where there had been buildings, there remained only gutted roofless structures, isolated chimneys, and heaps of rubble.

Throughout history, the Hungarians and the Poles have been close friends. We exchanged kings and fought side by side against the Turks and Tartars. John III Sobieski, King of Poland, saved Vienna from Turkish occupation. Nonetheless, Poland was on three occasions divided between Russia, Austria, and Prussia. In World War II, the luckless Poles were again brutalized and cheated – but not by us. Our troops played no part in repressing the historic Uprising of 1944. We Hungarians felt tremendous sympathy for the Free Poles. When their agents begged me for whatever aid we could spare, I talked to General Ibrányi, and he told me that I was free to help if I could find a way.

This much is certain: The Germans would have executed me, if they had caught me giving aid to the Free Poles. I would nonetheless place some medicine, radios, ammunition, and other necessities in a truck and would lead the way at night on my motorcycle to a chosen location. The partisans would be waiting for me in the dark, and I was always touched by their gratitude for the meager assistance that I was able to give them.

In Byelorussia and during the retreat to Warsaw, our division had suffered so many casualties that the Germans decided we were no longer combat effective. In early September, they sent us back to Hungary, which the Russians were about to invade. General Ibrányi, his chief of staff, I as the aide-de-camp, a good driver, and a sergeant with a machine gun set out for Budapest in a six-wheeled armored car. In order to get accurate information about what was happening in Hungary, I suggested that we return via Vienna, where my brother, Paul, was vice consul at the Hungarian Consulate. General Ibrányi agreed, and I left a message for Paul that three people would be arriving for luncheon.

The final battle for Eastern Europe was by then well underway. Hitler had commanded his generals to hold the two great cities of the East – Warsaw and Budapest – at all costs. Stalin had commanded his generals to take both. An irresistible force was colliding with an immovable object. As we journeyed south toward Vienna, the roads were crowded with thousands of troops heading in both directions.

At the Hungarian Consulate, Paul offered us a tasty, well-served luncheon and the whole political/military situation was discussed. We knew by then that the Axis was falling apart. On August 23rd, King Michael of Romania had swept his pro-German government from office and had ordered the arrest of his fascist prime minister, Ion Antonescu, who was later taken out and shot. In exchange, Stalin had agreed to an armistice with Romania.

Paul now informed us that our Regent, Admiral Horthy, was also scrambling to disengage from his misbegotten alliance with Hitler and was putting out feelers to the Russians for an armistice. With the fortunes of war tilting heavily against the Axis, Horthy had at last decided to risk all and remove our pro-German prime minister, General Sztójay, from office. He had then called General Géza Lakatos, an independent-minded nationalist, to head the

Warsaw after the Germans

Warsaw after the Germans

next government. If Horthy felt relieved at Hitler's failure to intervene, it was because he didn't know that the Führer had already devised a contingency plan for his removal from office, and Veesenmayer was standing by to carry it out. Horthy had also ordered the arrest of Ferenc Szálasi, the Hungarian fascist leader of the Arrow Cross Party, but the Germans were protecting him. Hitler was keeping Szálasi in reserve, as a replacement for Horthy. The Nazi dictator had grown weary of dealing with an ally who was more interested in making peace with the Russians than in killing them.

Ever since Stalingrad, most of us had believed that Hitler would lose the war, but it was not yet clear which of the Allied Powers would occupy the Eastern European countries, Hungary, Poland, Czechoslovakia, Romania, Bulgaria, and the Baltic States. We had hoped that Prime Minister Churchill's proposal to launch an Allied invasion from Italy into Central Europe before the Russians occupied it would be adopted by Britain and America. But this was not to be, and after President Roosevelt's ill-considered insistence, at Casablanca, on the unconditional surrender of Germany and her allies, many Eastern European leaders decided that there was nothing they could do to save their countries from eventual Soviet occupation. For the Germans, the only solution would have been to make peace with Russia, because Churchill and Roosevelt were not willing to join with Hitler in a war against Stalin.

Paul told us that the British and Americans had refused to negotiate with us, though we had good contacts in the neutral countries, namely Switzerland, Sweden, Spain, Portugal, and Turkey. We also learned that we could expect to be in the Soviet zone of occupation, which was devastating news.

I then accompanied General Ibrányi to Budapest, and we continued eastward to the front. What remained of our division was immediately ordered into battle – no rest, no refilling of the ranks.

When the Russians invaded Hungary in late September 1944, the Germans could raise no comparable force to oppose them. Much less could we. It was now obvious that our country would be overrun, and we were convinced that the invaders would remain.

In a last-ditch effort to avoid disaster, Horthy sent a secret emissary, General Gábor Faraghó, to Moscow to bargain for an armistice with the Russians, but Stalin's demand that Hungarian troops immediately open fire on the Germans was clearly unacceptable. Politically, it would have been impossible to implement, and militarily, it would have amounted to suicide. Moreover, Horthy's secret negotiations with the Soviet dictator were quickly discovered by German intelligence. The eyes and ears of Hitler were everywhere.

Fall of the Regent Horthy,
The Arrow Cross Fascists Seize Power,
Abduction of Raoul Wallenberg,
The Storming of Budapest

In the fateful second week of October 1944, an officer of the Guard arrived from the Royal Castle to announce that the Regent Horthy had ordered my commander, General Ibrányi, to report to him immediately. The general and I shaved, cleaned up, and left for Budapest in a hurry. At the Castle, anxiety and confusion prevailed. I waited in an antechamber while in the next room Horthy urgently conferred with the chief of the cabinet (Gyula Ambrozy), the defense minister (General Lajos Csatay), the chief of staff (General János Vörös), the commander of the Royal Guard (General Károly Lázár), my general, and the commanders of the First and Second Armies (Generals Béla Dálnoki-Miklós and Lajos Veres de Dálnoki). The meeting lasted until midnight. After that, my general insisted on "seeing" his wife, so it was 4 A.M. before we returned to the front. I didn't ask questions, but it was obvious that the military situation had become desperate and that the future of our country was hanging by a thread.

On October 15th, Horthy made his memorable radio address to the nation. In desperation, he proclaimed a "preliminary armistice" with the Russians, but since he could not possibly satisfy all of Stalin's outrageous demands, the armistice was essentially unilateral. Nonetheless, our generals and all other commanders were ordered to stop fighting so that Soviet troops could march through Hungary without destroying the country.

The speech was badly prepared and aroused a groundswell of indignation. Our soldiers refused to believe that they were being ordered to lay down their arms before the hated Soviet invaders. So the fighting went on, in spite of hopeless odds.

Events now took a sharp turn for the worse. Infuriated by Horthy's double-dealing, Hitler ordered his arrest and forced him to publicly retract his radio proclamation. That done, the Regent was made to abdicate. He was then packed off to Germany and thrown in jail. At the same time his younger son, Miki, was kidnapped, arrested at gunpoint, rolled up in a rug, and carried away as a hostage by the notorious SS commander, Otto Skorzeny, who had liberated Mussolini from his prison at Gran Sasso. Long after the war, I met Skorzeny in fascist Spain, where the dictator was protecting him. We had a lively conversation about the "good old days" that weren't so good. It turned out that Skorzeny was an Austrian – like Hitler.

The Regent Horthy was liberated by American troops at the end of the war. He was rigorously questioned by the International Military Tribunal at Nürnberg about his cynical alliance with Hitler, but he talked his way out of everything. Nothing could be made to stick to him, and his American interrogators may have learned that there is truth in the saying that only a Hungarian can enter a revolving door behind you and come out in front of you.

Horthy was eventually permitted to settle in Portugal, but his condition was pitiful. His elder son had been killed in Russia, his land in Hungary had been confiscated, and he was old and penniless. A number of compassionate Hungarian expatriates contributed to a fund that enabled him to buy a small house. I finally met him at Estoril, but our conversation amounted only to pleasantries. He died in 1957 at the age of 88. But back to my story.

After Horthy's arrest, the Germans pressured our parliament to install the fascist leader, Ferenc Szálasi, of the Arrow Cross Party, as Nemzetvezetvö, "Supreme Leader" or "Führer" of Hungary. That Szálasi was the last Hungarian ruler to call for diehard resistance to the Russian invasion has earned him a grudging measure of respect from present-day Hungarians. But nothing can exonerate him for the innumerable summary executions and other crimes for which he was eventually hanged.

Meanwhile, Soviet troops continued to pour across the Tisza River, and by November we were fighting only ten miles from Budapest. Someone threw a hand grenade into the room where General Ibrányi and his staff were conferring, and he was severely wounded in the head. The staff decided that I should drive him to a hospital in western Hungary, and after a hectic journey, I managed to bring him there alive, but the doctors gave him only a 50 percent chance of surviving.

It was my duty to return to the front immediately. In our family, it would have been unthinkable for anyone to desert, and I would never have done so under any circumstances. That said, the war was obviously lost, and I had obligations to my family. For the time being, Paul was safe at our consulate in Vienna, and my mother, my sister, and her family were still safe on their farms in Somogy County. But our new regime, which consisted of

My military decorations

Nazi sympathizers, had sent my father to a concentration camp for nothing more than his moderate political views. I was in no hurry to die for this kind of a government! And since General Ibrányi owed me a favor, I asked him to discharge me from the army. My military papers consisted of a small booklet, which every officer carried. At the end was a discharge document which my commander could sign to release me from service. The general may have saved my life when he graciously signed this document. Unfortunately, the Russians eventually captured him, and he suffered for eight years in Soviet concentration camps.

From my friends at the Foreign Office, I now learned that four or five leading diplomats had already been arrested by our fascist government on orders from the Germans. Having made no secret of my dislike for fascism, I was now in danger myself, and it was clearly impossible for me to return to the diplomatic corps. My former colleagues understood this. They gave me a diplomatic passport and wished me good luck.

For the next few months I lived inconspicuously, moving often and keeping a low profile. I gave my flat to a group of people who needed it for English, French and Polish refugees who were attempting to escape via Croatia to southern Italy and North Africa. My friend Baroness Anna Harkány then permitted me to rent in a building that faced the main square of Pest and was three blocks east of the Danube. The Wagons-Lits company, whose president was my friend Prince Franzi Hohenlohe, also rented in that building.

The short-lived Szálasi regime, which Hitler supported enthusiastically, was opposed by a number of anti-fascist groups that went "underground". My cousin Gene de Thassy, who had obtained a discharge from the army by faking tuberculosis, belonged to one of these groups. It also included my friend Freddy Lippe, a German aristocrat who had only contempt for the Nazis. I collaborated with these two friends in an effort to help foreigners, Jews, and other civilians who faced imprisonment or death from Arrow Cross hoodlums and their handlers, the Germans.

Sam Stern, the principal rabbi of Budapest, would come to us with lists of Jewish individuals and families who needed protection, and we would try to help. In the course of these efforts, I became a friend of Rabbi Stern's.

Another frequent visitor was Raoul Wallenberg, a 32-year-old attaché who had arrived at the neutral Swedish Embassy in Budapest with a diplomatic passport signed by King Gustav himself. I worked closely with Wallenberg. He would issue a "protection pass," stating that So-and-So was under the protection of the Royal Swedish Embassy. Today, Raoul Wallenberg is a hero because thousands of Hungarian Jews escaped extermination, thanks to his intervention. But fate dealt harshly with him.

Wallenberg, who knew almost nothing about Hungary, needed us for information that would help him distribute his protection passes. I found him to be pleasant, courageous, helpful, and gentlemanly, but he was overworked, overwrought, and had started to drink heavily. In January 1945, the Soviet

My friend Sam Stern, the chief rabbi of Budapest, whom our group attempted to help

Raoul Wallenberg, who would visit our group for assistance in distributing his protection passes

authorities ordered him to appear at a command post in Pest. We advised him not to go. He insisted that nothing could happen to him; Sweden was a neutral country and he had a diplomatic passport signed by the king himself. We told him, in so many words, that he was naïve and inexperienced about Soviet matters and that his extraordinary passport might even count against him. He nonetheless kept his appointment with the Russians and disappeared forever into the tangle of Stalin's prisons and concentration camps. Decades would pass before the particulars of his end came to light. Suspected of espionage, Wallenberg was arrested and transferred to Moscow. On July 17, 1947, he was murdered in the infamous Lubianka prison, allegedly by lethal injection, and obviously with Stalin's consent, if not at his insistence.

It was at this time that Countess Ilona Esterházy entered my life. Lilly, as everyone called her, had married a delightful and amusing friend of mine, Miki Cziráky. He had served with me in the army and had asked me to look after his wife if he were killed.

Lilly had already suffered a severe shock. She had become pregnant, and her family had sent her to the country, where they thought she would be safe and could relax. But the pilot of an incapacitated American bomber had released his bombs, and one had struck the castle in which Lilly was resting. She lost her child. Then, in September 1944, she also lost her husband, who was killed fighting the Russians. I searched for Lilly after the fall of Budapest, and she became the only girl to whom I have ever been engaged, apart from my wife. But more about Lilly in a moment.

On Christmas Eve of 1944, some friends invited me to celebrate with them at their home on the outskirts of Budapest. I was rattling along on a streetcar when suddenly I noticed peculiar-looking soldiers hiding behind trees. They were Russians. I ran to the conductor and told him to reverse and race back to the city. A couple of phone calls confirmed that Budapest had become the front.

On the following day, Christmas, there was street fighting and an artillery barrage. The apartment house where I was staying was damaged, and our little group of fugitives gathered hurriedly in the cellar. Expecting the worst, we had already bought a supply of flour, ham, salami, potatoes, coffee, tea, preserves, toilet paper, candles, and matches for our own use and to exchange for other necessities. We broke our bottles of wine and liquor, as we knew what it would mean to have drunken Soviet soldiers hanging around. We were sharing our cellar with the head of the Benedictine Order, who said prayers for us every evening, two friends from the Foreign Office, and an attractive girl from one of the nightclubs. In the adjoining cellar was my cousin Gene de Thassy, as well as Freddy Lippe, the Malagola family from Italy, and other friends. We broke down the door between the two cellars and formed a jolly little group. We had bridge and poker parties, though there was no running water, no electricity, no heat, no telephone, and no toilet facilities. When our bottled water ran out, I and the other young bachelors would walk to the Danube at night and fetch river water, which then had to be boiled. One of the women gave birth, which greatly complicated our lives. All of us slept on mattresses. One corner of the cellar served as the W.C. Luckily, we had enough chalk to disinfect it.

The Russians stormed Budapest with 177,000 troops commanded by Marshal Rodion Malinovsky. The German defenders numbered only 79,000 and were woefully deficient in tanks, artillery and aircraft, but to hold our capital city they fought for 51 days with a ferocity that was almost superhuman. They knew that if Budapest fell to the Russians, Vienna would fall next, and then Berlin.

The crash and thunder of artillery bombardments left us completely nerve-racked. Without warning, the walls of our cellar would shake with giant explosions as the Germans brawled with the Russians. But somehow life went on. We were young, had something to eat, played at cards, and were surrounded by friends. We laughed a great deal and tried to help people who were desperate. We didn't take life very seriously, because we didn't know how long it would last. People died and we would have to bury them, though the ground was frozen and heavily blanketed in snow.

Our fascist government took to its heels, and the Hungarian "Führer", Szálasi, fled to western Hungary. The police and fire departments ceased to function, and there were no doctors. Gangs of Arrow Cross killers stalked the streets, shooting their perceived opponents or hanging them from lamp posts. But even in these surreal circumstances, we were determined to remain brave and cheerful and to live life with a kind of defiant flair. We were, after all, Europeans.

When we ran out of meat, we shot a sick horse, dragged it to the Wagons-Lits office on the ground floor of our building, and covered it with snow. Every day, each of us got a *côtelette,* and we gave some meat to our friends. One morning the carcass was gone, but we didn't have to shoot another horse, because by then the battle for Pest was nearly over. Across the river, in Buda, the inevitable Russian victory was delayed for three more weeks because the Germans had blown up the bridges over the Danube. On February 11, 1945, the guns at last fell silent. Thirty-eight thousand German troops and many thousands of Hungarian civilians had been killed. Our beautiful capital was a gutted, blasted shambles.

After the fighting in Pest, drunken Soviet soldiers burned our cellar. We had to evacuate everybody, but no one was hurt. People were extremely helpful and generous. The iron loyalty that Hungarians show toward one another in desperate times is perhaps our most admirable quality. Everybody had a friend to go to. I went to the house of some friends who lived 200 meters away. Their doorway was completely bombed out, and I could hardly find my way to the cellar, but when I got down there, I discovered a very amusing and fun-loving group. The owner had dug a well in the cellar before the battle, so this group had its own water supply. There were no strangers in that cellar, so the group brought in French wine and boxes of fine food. They were wonderfully organized! I was accepted with great hospitality and given a toothbrush and razor. When a friend of mine who was a dentist arrived with a drill that had to be operated with a foot pedal, I was given a white coat with a red cross on it and, in Russian, the word "dentist". I would stand in my new uniform in front of the house, and if Soviet soldiers wanted to enter, I would show them papers saying that we were dentists. The soldiers who asked to have gold crowns put on their teeth were told to bring the gold. They didn't trust us and wouldn't allow us to give them injections against pain. Can you imagine what they suffered??? I foot-pedaled the machine, and the dentist drilled not only their teeth but also their gums, saying in Hungarian, "This is for the raped girls, to whom you also gave venereal diseases."

The rapes were the most terrible punishments of the Russian invasion. Young girls, expectant mothers, even women in the hospitals – no one was spared once the Soviets got drunk. Venereal diseases and ordinary infections were rampant, because we were living in filthy conditions and no one could get penicillin.

A seventy-year-old woman told us her story. Six Russian soldiers had raped her, one at a time, while the others watched, holding their rifles in readiness so that no one could interfere. At one point, her face flared up, and she remarked what a good-looking boy the number four rapist had been.

While I was a dentist's assistant, I caught typhoid, and nobody was allowed to see me; the illness was very contagious, and no effective medicine was available. My comrades pushed some food across to me, but my dentist friend said that I wouldn't live very long, in any case.

I sent a message to my dear friend, Erzsébet Ullmann, and said good-bye to her. To my great astonishment, she came and said that she would cure me. She stayed for two weeks and probably saved my life. She was one of the most courageous and wonderful girls I have ever known.

After taking Budapest, the Russians overran the rest of Hungary in two months, and ironically they liberated my father from the fascist concentration camp where Arrow Cross hoodlums had imprisoned him for four months. The Russians even reinstated him as county executive of Somogy, correctly assuming that a man whom the people respected would be able to keep order there.

After that, my parents continued to live on our farm with more than fifteen elderly ladies – relatives, friends, and neighbors

– who were all over seventy and were staying with us as refugees. Mother was the only younger woman, and she dressed like a man to avoid problems with the Soviet soldiers, who came regularly to look for girls, alcohol, and food, in that order.

She told me how, on one occasion, two nice-looking young Russian soldiers came with two fish that they had caught and were still alive. Looking around, they found water for the fish in the W.C. All went well until they started playing with the handle of the toilet and the water and fish disappeared. The Russians grabbed up their guns and shouted, "Sabotage! Where are the fish?" Poor boys, they had never seen a toilet. Imagine how difficult it was to explain, without speaking Russian, where the fish had gone.

The Soviet army then invaded Austria, and three days before it occupied Vienna, Princess Gabrielle of Liechtenstein, who was in love with my brother, Paul, hid him in the trunk of her diplomatic car and smuggled him into Switzerland with the luggage. A year later, when the war ended, Paul returned to Hungary and I helped him resume his diplomatic career. In 1946, he was appointed first secretary of the Hungarian Embassy in Prague.

After the war, the Allied Control Commission for Hungary was established to supervise the occupation of our country and to direct its political reconstruction. General Geoffrey Keyes and General Edgecomb were the American and British representatives on the Commission, but decisive power rested in the hands of its president, Stalin's drinking companion, Marshal Klementiy Voroshilov. More important, the Russian army was to remain as the sole occupying force in Hungary, and it would take orders only from Voroshilov. Thus we found ourselves in the Soviet sphere of influence and under Russian military control – the nightmare every Hungarian had dreaded. Moreover, a crowd of Soviet agents who had followed the Russian troops into Hungary began to agitate for a Stalinist state. Nevertheless, the political subversion of our country by the communists was surprisingly gradual.

At this time a great friend of mine, Béla Cziráky, the brother of Miki whom I've already mentioned, was a prisoner-of-war in Russian captivity. His uncle, Count Mihály Károlyi, a former president of Hungary, tried to arrange for Béla's release. He appealed to Marshal Voroshilov, who responded graciously: "What is your nephew's number?" Every prisoner had a number; the Russians didn't bother with names. Béla's mother had to sign a receipt confirming that she had received, from the Soviet officer who returned her son, one young man with curly brown hair and a tooth missing.

Back to the Foreign Office

By the fall of 1945, the political situation had begun to stabilize. Elections for a new Hungarian parliament were held in November, and while the communists had all the necessary money and backing from Moscow, as well as control of the army and police, they won only 12 percent of the vote. Though the new government immediately confiscated about 200 of our family's 900 acres, some of us were, at first, cautiously optimistic about the future.

What did the most to brighten my life was finding Lilly, the widow of my friend Miki Cziráky, who had been killed in the war. I was honor-bound to take care of Lilly, and I did. We fell in love, moved into a little flat, and were blissfully happy.

After the war, there was a desperate need for money and workmen to restore our hospitals and schools and to provide office space for the new government and for the Allied Control Commission (ACC). Having decided to resume my diplomatic career, I met with my former colleagues every day in the bombed and burned-out Hungarian Foreign Office. It could almost be said that our ministry had ceased to exist. But then someone from the government came around and told us that our new headquarters would be on Liberty Square, quite close to the Swiss and American legations. At this new location, we started to clean out and paint some rooms. We put in desks, restored the electricity, and installed telephones. In three to four months, the new Hungarian Foreign Office began to function.

As I spoke a number of languages and was in every way qualified, my new job was to serve as liaison officer to the British and American sections of the ACC. A large number of diplomats needed houses, flats, food, and petrol for their cars. As I attempted to help everyone in the Anglo-Saxon community, I came to feel like a real estate agent, handyman, and nanny rolled into one. I made many friends. From the principal American doctor, Colonel Harry McCain, I managed to get penicillin for the girls who had been raped by the Russians.

In the summer of 1946, I received a letter from England saying that a young British diplomat would soon arrive from Cairo to take up the post of political officer at the British section of the ACC. His name was Peter Stirling, and he was said to like women, riding, and shooting. Peter arrived, and I introduced him to some attractive girls. I also arranged for him to join the riding school I had started outside Budapest for the diplomats, and I began to organize bird shooting for the fall. Peter became a lifelong friend of mine, and eventually so would his eldest brother, Colonel Bill Stirling.

Meanwhile, the Hungarian government was becoming steadily more socialistic, aggressive, and unpredictable. The communists, who were in charge of internal security, detained my father for his liberal political views, just as the fascists had done, so once again he was behind wire, and there was absolutely nothing we could do to get him out.

And when our corn crop could not be harvested on time because there were not enough farm workers, my mother was put in jail, at Kaposvár, in the same building where she and my father had formerly occupied the executive apartment. She asked the other prisoners, who were mostly prostitutes, to turn their backs while she was washing herself with cold water. For that "arrogant" request, she was made to scrub the floor of the prison while "les girls" looked on in amusement and disbelief. She was finally released, and the chief of police at Kaposvár, who knew who she was, apologized and assisted her in every way.

Though the largest estates had been nationalized and most of my friends were living in utter poverty, there was excellent habitat for shooting in Hungary, and a number of former landowners collaborated with me to organize challenging drives for pheasants and partridges. Since Hungarians were not permitted to own firearms, I found some hidden guns and gave them to various shooting members of the ACC. I then invited my Hungarian friends to shoot with us, and we began to have some real fun, thanks to the foreign diplomats. On Hansi Meran's estate, we shot over a thousand cock pheasants a day with eight to ten guns. We also had wonderful shooting on the former estate of my lifelong friend Feri Széchenyi.

During one of these shoots, there was a heavy fog, and we did not realize that the Russians were shooting over the same territory. As they had machine guns and hand grenades, they arrested all of us, including the English diplomats. We spent the night in dirty rooms without heating or food until the following morning, when the Russians realized that some of our group were diplomats and members of the ACC. We Hungarians were pleased; the Anglo-Saxons were at last able to see what was happening in our country.

I was eventually sent with the diplomatic bag to London and Paris. That was my first trip to these storied cities, and it made a lasting impression on me. In London, I was introduced to some interesting politicians and members of the leading families by Judith, Countess of Listowel, who was Hungarian by birth and a former neighbor of ours. A letter of introduction was also awaiting me from Count László Széchenyi, who had been the minister of our embassy in London before the war and whose wife, born Gladys Vanderbilt, owned the famous mansion the Breakers at Newport, Rhode Island.

I thoroughly enjoyed my first visit to Britain, but there was no danger of my remaining there because my entire family was still in Hungary.

In 1947, the Hungarian government, which by then was heavily infiltrated by communists, began to confiscate all private property – real estate, industry, banks and utilities – without compensation. Most of our farmland was impounded that year. As a veteran of World War II and a member of the anti-fascist underground, I was at first permitted to keep 300 acres, but even that was soon taken away.

About the same time, an American delegation arrived in Budapest on its way to Moscow. It included a young, very handsome congressman who became a friend of mine and played a very important role in my future. His name was John Davis Lodge, and he belonged to the prominent Boston family of that name. He would later become governor of Connecticut and ambassador to Spain, Switzerland, and Argentina.

Permit me to quote from *John Davis Lodge, A Life in Three Acts,* by Thomas de Long, which records my first meeting with this distinguished American:

"John Lodge, now accompanied by Senator Alben Barkley, was met at the airport in Budapest by U.S. Minister Selden Chaplin and driven immediately to meet the Hungarian President, Dr. Zoltan Tildy. Hungary's Foreign Office staff included a young liaison officer to the U.S. and British sections of the Allied Control

Commission, Dr. Peter Stephaich. He was assigned to take Lodge by automobile to an official reception later that day. En route the car broke down. Stephaich, a staunch anti-communist, brusquely pushed Lodge out of the vehicle and instructed the Hungarian driver: 'You fix this car. I will take this American gentleman to the dinner party by taxi.'

"The problem with the car gave Stephaich a few hurried minutes to speak to Lodge without being overheard by any assigned drivers. 'All our drivers are secret service police officers and can't be trusted,' Stephaich whispered as they waited for a cab. 'Your entire agenda is for show – a total fake. It is all arranged, complete with caviar and champagne, to give you Americans the impression that democracy is coming rapidly to Hungary. But it is just the opposite. The Soviets have overrun the country and are really in control.'

"'Why should I believe you?' asked John.

"'Tomorrow, Mr. Lodge, we are going to see an iron works. The men in charge will tell you in so many words that free enterprise prevails and all is fine and wonderful. Actually, many at the plant have been thrown into prison by the communist regime, and the Russian grip is getting tighter. I know the speech well – I helped to write it – and it is all false.'

"Later at the reception, Stephaich and Lodge managed a brief exchange of words: 'If you ever need anything and run into a serious situation, Peter, let me know. I will remember your name and will try to help you.' John left word at the American Legation about Stephaich, who proved right about the rigged itinerary and the serious inroads by the communists.

"Later, as the communist purges intensified during the winter of 1947-48, Peter passed a message to the U.S. Legation that he might need to flee Hungary. Would they help once he left the country? Then, on the eve of his marriage in Budapest, a friend from the Foreign Office informed Peter that he would be arrested the next morning. Without wasting a minute, he bolted from the country with only the clothes on his back. He headed to Prague, where his brother was first secretary of the Hungarian Embassy, then to Rome. Through Lodge's intervention, Peter, in order to gain admittance to the States, took a State Department exam as an 'agricultural specialist'. In America his first job was milking cows in New Jersey. Lodge again helped Stephaich. He prepared special legislation to grant U.S. citizenship to ex-diplomats."

Marriage Plans

After the departure of the American delegation, Lilly and I started to think seriously about our future. I had always believed that it would eventually be impossible for us to stay in Hungary. With good contacts and money, one could get an exit visa to leave the country, and many of our friends had already left. Lilly was an Esterházy by birth, and her family had been the foremost landowners in Hungary, but their estates had all been confiscated without compensation. I had a job in the Foreign Office, but since my brother was serving at our embassy in Prague, I knew that the government would not give me a position abroad, for they would have no guarantee that Paul and I would return. I also had to consider that it was impossible to live on a Foreign Office salary.

The Anglo-Saxon diplomats whom we saw daily were persuaded that we in Hungary would have to live under Soviet rule. But when you're young, you're optimistic, and if you're also in love, as we were, you're not completely rational.

Lilly and I finally decided to get married. The date was to be January 28, 1948. We got our witnesses. I asked Paul to be my best man.

Then, literally one day before our marriage, an employee at the Foreign Office, for whom I had once done a great favor, told me very discreetly that I should not go home that night because the secret police were coming to my flat at 7 A.M. They would confiscate my diplomatic passport and would then arrest me. He told me that a great purge was about to take place and that it would be directed against those who had not yet joined the Communist Party.

I arranged for a civil marriage that night, but on my parents' advice I canceled these plans because once married to me, Lilly would not be allowed to leave Hungary. I decided to use my diplomatic passport and depart at once for Prague, where I could discuss my future and Lilly's with my brother. I phoned Paul and told him not to come to Budapest – wedding postponed.

Around 3 A.M., I called on the American ambassador. He had a vice- consul named Al Bentley, who was later killed by a bomb in Washington D.C., and it was Bentley who gave me the exam that qualified me for a non quota special immigration visa to enter the United States.

It was terrible to say goodbye to my family and to my beloved country. Wearing white gloves and carrying a small suitcase, I traveled first class on the train to Prague with tears in my eyes. I told Lilly that once I arrived in Rome, Paris, or London, I would get her a visitor's visa and we could get married and go to the U.S.A.

My trip to Prague was easy. Paul was waiting for me at the station, and he deposited me in the flat of Fabrizio Franco, the first secretary of the Italian Embassy. I could not go to the Hungarian Embassy for obvious reasons. We discussed our future. Paul had also decided to leave the Foreign Office and wanted to go to South America because it was easy to get an immigration visa and he liked the Latins. He chose Argentina, where our good friend Géza Pejacsevich had become the secret lover of Evita Perón, the dictator's wife. I had always wanted to go to the United States and left for Rome to wait for my U.S. visa.

In Rome, my friends were very helpful and hospitable. Dr. Ted Sedlmayr, my grandmother's brother, had been living in America since 1905. I called him from Prague and told him my plans. He was very kind and helpful. Uncle Ted had an important position in a company called Standard Brands, which was controlled by the Fleischman family and was listed on the New York Stock Exchange.

Through friends in the Italian Foreign Office, I got a visa for Lilly, and she arrived in Rome a few months later. Meanwhile, I applied for an agricultural immigration visa to the U.S.A.

One day, diving into the swimming pool at the San Giorgio Club in Rome, my knee got blocked, and I couldn't straighten it out. My good and clever friends, sitting on my body, forced my knee and tore the cartilage. I needed an operation. One of these friends knew a young doctor who had never performed a knee operation but who was willing to operate free. So I spent a week in a terrible hospital and then limped for a few more weeks. That knee has troubled me all my life. Luckily, Lilly had arrived by then and helped me through my convalescence. I stayed with different friends, and everyone was more than helpful and kind.

We planned to get married in Rome, but there was a law that one Hungarian citizen could only marry another with permission from the Ministry of the Interior in Budapest. We argued that we were refugees and that the communist government would never grant us this permission. But the law was the law. We wanted to get married only in church, but without a license issued by the state, our marriage would not be legally valid in America.

We decided that once I had my American resident's visa, now called a "green card", I would obtain a visitor's visa for Lilly. We could then go to Cuba or Canada, get married there, and return legally to the U.S.A.

I Arrive in America

My U.S. immigration visa was issued in September 1948. The next problem was how to get to America with no money. Again, one of my friends in Italy helped me. Countess Mary Roberti, a U.S. citizen married to a senior Italian diplomat, got me a ticket from Palermo, Sicily, to Newport News, Virginia, on a freighter. I had to do odd jobs on board during the trip, but I was happy. Everything looked promising for my future in America.

The journey lasted about six weeks, as we stopped at different ports in Africa to unload cargo. When we arrived at Newport News, a doctor asked for my chest X ray. I did not know what that was. In Europe, we called it a Röntgen. During the trip, a law had been passed that every immigrant arriving in America had to have a chest X ray, so that tuberculosis would not enter the country.

I was therefore confined to a naval hospital and placed in a large ward with maybe a hundred beds. There was only one other man in the ward. He sat on my bed and kept telling me that all the other occupants were crazy and that I had to be very careful. There was nobody else in sight, but this man kept insisting. Finally, I went to the guard and asked him to give me a chair in another room, as I didn't want to spend the night with a lunatic. So I spent my entire first night in America sitting in a chair. The guard assured me that on Monday a doctor would come and clear up my problem, but it was only Saturday. On Monday the doctor did arrive, made his examination, discharged me, and wished me good luck.

I went to the nearest bar and asked for a whisky and soda. I wanted to celebrate. The bartender said, "This is a dry county." I waited patiently, and after a while I asked again for my whisky. The barman replied, "I've already told you, this is a dry county." I asked him what the lack of rain had to do with my whisky. He just looked at me, and we soon straightened out our misunderstanding. I learned that in some counties they didn't serve alcohol, or only during certain hours. I told him stories about Hungary, and we became friends. I asked him how I could get to New York City in the cheapest possible way. "Greyhound bus," he replied. But I did not have enough money for the ticket, so I left my gold wristwatch with him. Once in New York, I would send him the money and he would send me my watch. After a long bus trip, I arrived in New York, at Grand Central Station. My final destination was 1000 Park Avenue, at 84th Street, where the Weiss and Chorin families – Hungarians all – had nice apartments. I thought that 42nd Street and 84th Street couldn't be very far from each other, so I started to walk carrying my suitcase. It took me quite a while, and I arrived completely exhausted. Baron Jenö Weiss and Dr. Ferenc Chorin were more than kind and generous to me. I have loved them ever since. Uncle Ted sent me some money, and I reclaimed my wristwatch from the bartender in Newport News.

The next step was to find a job and get my papers in order. I explained my situation to Dr. Ludd Spivey, whom I had met in Rome and who was the president of Florida Southern College, in Lakeland. He suggested I come and join him. As I didn't have any winter clothes, his invitation was tempting, and I finally accepted it on the advice of Uncle Ted and Dr. Chorin. Again, the Greyhound – this time to Florida.

It was about then that I phoned my friend, John Lodge, who told me that my immigrant visa was ready and that I was a resident of the United States.

The campus of Florida Southern College looked very friendly and rich. That it had been built by Frank Lloyd Wright meant nothing to me.

"With a Ph.D. you don't get anywhere," Dr. Spivey told me. He suggested that I work in the garden, be a model for painting classes, or do other odd jobs. He also told me that a young couple whom I would like would soon be arriving.

The lovely young couple arrived. Emlen Etting gave painting lessons and his wife, Gloria Bragiotti, gave ballet classes. It turned out that Gloria was the sister of Mrs. Lodge – an unbelievable coincidence. We became lifelong friends.

In the meantime my fiancée, Lilly, had received her papers for a student visa through Dr. Spivey, and she applied for it at the U.S. Embassy in Rome. An idiot told her that he knew the U.S. ambassador well and that he could get her a visitor's visa immediately. Poor Lilly applied for the visitor's visa and found herself in a hopeless situation: U.S. law held that a person who had applied for two kinds of visas at the same time was obviously engaging in a subterfuge and could not enter the United States. I was heartbroken and desperate. Unfortunately, that was the end of our wedding plans.

Lilly eventually married Prince Constantine of Liechtenstein. Today, she and I are in our late eighties, but we keep in touch and will always be friends.

In Palm Beach, Philadelphia, and New York

One day, Gloria Etting told me that, since her uncle Atwater Kent's death, his widow, Aunt Mabel, who lived in Palm Beach, had been very lonesome. Gloria asked if I would be willing to keep her aunt company and promised to get permission for me from Dr. Spivey. I had never heard of Palm Beach but was soon told that it was a nice place and that the Kents were good people. Dr. Spivey encouraged me to go, for by then he no longer knew what to do with me.

So I went to Palm Beach and found the Kents living in a cottage called "Nautilus". This was the first and best cottage at the

Breakers Hotel, on the ocean. Mrs. Kent, her French daughter-in-law, and her granddaughter, Suzanne, lived in this cottage in great luxury. I had a wonderful time. Little Suzanne, a lovely blonde child about seven years old and with two teeth missing, became a great friend of mine. About fifteen years later, she became my sister-in-law when she married Tommy Hitchcock III, my wife's brother. Again, what a coincidence.

Gloria also introduced me to a family named Lloyd, who lived outside Philadelphia on the Main Line, which again meant nothing to me. But I became a close friend of Lallie Lloyd's, and she invited me to visit her family in Philadelphia. Fortunately, when I returned to Lakeland, the Ettings were still there. Without them, life at the College would have been very dull.

Dr. Spivey now informed me that his Italian professor had resigned and that I was to give Italian lessons to seven or eight students. Having met me in Rome, he assumed that I was fluent in Italian, when in fact I knew only a few words. Fearing to disappoint him, I agreed to give the lessons, but believe me, I considered very carefully what I was going to tell my students the next morning! There was no problem until one day a curious girl asked me, "How do you say Merry Christmas in Italian?" I was not prepared for this question and immediately dismissed the class. I went to Dr. Spivey and told him that I could no longer serve as his Italian professor because I didn't speak Italian. He agreed.

By spring, I decided that I had been Dr. Spivey's protégé long enough. So I went back to New York and arranged to share a flat with my cousin Gene de Thassy, who now lived conveniently close to 1000 Park Avenue, where my friends lived. I had to find a job quickly, and once again Mary Roberti helped me. Through her, I received an invitation from a banker named Reeve Schley, who lived in New Jersey and was giving a black tie dinner dance that Saturday. I consulted Uncle Ted's checkbook and accepted.

Close to Bloomingdale's store on Lexington Avenue was a place where I rented an appropriate outfit for $20.

I was seated at the host's table, being the only foreigner and a protégé of Mary Roberti's. I felt a little lost at first, but a couple of whiskies revived me. Mr. Schley was complaining about a difficult problem he had. His cowhand had just quit, and he needed someone to take care of his Jersey cattle. I told him that I knew a man who would be perfect for the job. He was thrilled and told me to send him the new cowhand on Monday at 8 A.M.

On Sunday, I went back to New York and somehow found an open store where I bought blue jeans, boots, and a pullover – all that a cowhand needs – and reported to Mr. Schley at 8 A.M. on Monday.

He asked me, "Where's the cowhand?" I replied, "He's standing in front of you." Mr. Schley was embarrassed and did not want to hire me, but I talked him into it. I had a job! And I worked overtime on Sundays because I had to send money to my family in Budapest.

After a few weeks, my knee which had been operated on in Rome started to swell, and I had to find other work. I called my dear Hungarian friend Count Béla Hadik, whose wife had just bought a house at Chester, New Hampshire, from her cousin Bill Vanderbilt. They very kindly invited me to stay with them, and since they had a lot of work to do on their house, I became an assistant bricklayer. I had to join a union, and we were allowed to lay only four hundred bricks a day. But I was through working by about 2 P.M., and would go out with a gun and the Hadiks' Hungarian vizsla dogs to shoot woodcocks. I had a wonderful time with these kind and hospitable friends. Count Hadik's father, János, had been minister president of Hungary, and he became famous for having said, "A turkey is a very stupid bird: One turkey is not enough for a man; two turkeys are too much."

When the Hadiks' house was refurbished, I returned to my cousin's flat in New York. By then, the U.S. government had started a program called Radio Free Europe, with headquarters in New York and a large office in Munich, Germany. Cousin Gene was a scriptwriter there and arranged for me to become a radio announcer, broadcasting to Hungary.

Initially, the broadcasts to the Iron Curtain countries were challenging. I visited the Lloyds regularly in Pennsylvania and met many well-connected people there. Most of them had worked for the OSS (Office of Strategic Services), headed by General Bill Donovan, during the war or later for the Central Intelligence Agency, headed by Allen Dulles. Meeting these people, I realized how naïve the Americans were and how little they knew about Eastern and Central Europe. It was also evident that the U.S. was not interested in a part of the world that it had permitted the Soviets to subvert and take over without resistance. It took America a long time to realize that communism was more international and therefore more dangerous than Nazism. My days with the Lloyds were very pleasant, but I was disappointed by the intelligence operatives I met through them. Some of them failed to understand how I could still be alive if I was both anti-Nazi and anti-communist.

I called John Lodge and discussed the foregoing matters with him. He made an appointment for me to meet with a very pleasant and intelligent man, David Bruce, who gave me a CIA clearance at the end of a year and a half.

I moved quite often in those uncertain days. At one point, I was given the use of a flat by my English friend Roy Panett and occupied it with my dear Hungarian friend Gyuri Ullmann, the brother of Erzsébet. At that time, I was seeing quite a number of girls. I played tennis regularly with Cristina Torlonia, who was rather eccentric. We played at the River Club in New York and at the Piping Rock Club on Long Island. Her sister, Marina, would become the grandmother of Brooke Shields, the movie star. Cristina was a great friend of Barbara Hutton, the "poor little rich girl," who by then was spending most of her time drinking in bed at the Hotel Pierre.

There was one really attractive young girl, named Minola Habsburg. I was extremely fond of her, and she introduced me to her mother, Princess Ileane, the sister of King Carol II of Romania. Needless to say, she and I were not in the same league. Minola was an archduchess of Austria and a member of the imperial family, and I was an immigrant with no title. I also had no money. Minola eventually married a Czech count, and they were killed, a year later, in an airplane accident near Rio de Janeiro.

At that time, a German friend of mine, Goli Hohenberg, had a small house on Long Island, complete with swimming pool and tennis court. Our group of expatriates spent nearly all our weekends there. We ate spaghetti twice a day and drank vodka because it was cheap. Nobody had money, but this was the meeting place of the attractive international set – Henry of Bavaria, Johnny Pálffy, Didi Kesselstatt, Peter Salm, all the White Russians, and the young foreigners who lived in New York or were passing through. We had a very sporty life and spent the evenings beside a big bonfire with a guitar and singing.

Another rendezvous on Long Island for the young international set was the house of Pista Ráth, the same man for whom I had worked as a dentist's assistant in Budapest, after the Russian conquest, and with whose lovely daughter, Szuszi, I had enjoyed some oriental hospitality. I found this house for Pista, with its tennis court and swimming pool. For us young Europeans, it was an unheard of luxury.

And nearby was the home of Peter Salm, a superb thousand-acre estate on Peconic Bay, near Southampton. I eventually succeeded at bringing my friends the Nádosy family out of Austria, and with Móric Nádosy's advice we started, on Peter's estate, the only English-style driven pheasant shoot in America. The birds flew well, and bags of 300 to 400 a day were not uncommon.

Peter's estate, the Port of Missing Men, did not miss men because, with Peter's hospitality, it was always full of guests. And there was never a lack of good-looking girls, as Peter was one of the most eligible bachelors in America. He cultivated a highly civilized lifestyle and was both a charming and loyal friend. His early death saddened his numerous friends. We continue to miss him.

Enter Louise

About five years after I came to America, the Lloyd family gave a large delightful ball at Haverford, Pennsylvania. Afterwards, they asked me to chaperon to New York by train a nice blond girl named Louise Hitchcock, and I dropped her off at 10 Gracie Square, in Manhattan. About a year later, a cousin of the Bragiottis asked me to accompany her to a dinner party, as her date was unable to come. I accepted with pleasure without knowing where we were going. It turned out that we went to 10 Gracie Square, and there was Louise. She looked lovely, was full of fun, and we had a good laugh about the coincidence. I started to see her regularly. After a few months of falling in love and meeting her charming family, we were quite serious about making a future together. I told her frankly that my financial situation amounted to zero. Louise helped me get a job with American Export Lines, a steamship company that operated in the Mediterranean, the Middle East, and India. The company owned two 30,000-ton luxury liners, the *Independence* and the *Constitution*. My job was not very exciting, but every beginning is tedious. Eventually, I hoped to be able to find work abroad so that we could live in Europe.

I began to learn about Louise's family. Her father, Thomas Hitchcock, Jr., had been a hero in both world wars and had died at the age of forty-three while test-flying a fighter-bomber. He had been a ten-goal polo player for sixteen consecutive years and was unquestionably the best player in America. His father had also been a ten-goaler. The family had a lovely house in Westbury, Long Island, with every modern convenience. Louise had two very amusing, fun-loving younger brothers and a very attractive and intelligent younger sister. Louise's mother, Margaret Mellon Hitchcock, was a charming lady from Pittsburg.

I must tell you a lovely story that touched me very deeply. The prominent Wall Street banker, Bobby Lehman, who was a friend of Louise's family, invited me to luncheon at his bank. He said, "I know you intend to get married, but you will have a financial problem, as Louise's family is well off and you have very little. So let me give you a present of a hundred thousand dollars. That would be easy for me, and it would help you to start a new life." I was profoundly touched and could not say anything for a moment, as I was hardly able to hold back my tears. I then told this kind gentleman that I couldn't possibly accept his generous gift, as I had unfortunately been brought up not to accept money from other people. I wrote him a nice letter and we became lifelong friends.

Our Marriage

Eventually, we decided to get married. I invited Louise's mother to her favorite restaurant, Passy, and asked for permission to marry her daughter. She graciously agreed, and we talked about the future. I told her that I had lost all of my worldly possessions, and while I was determined to work, I would be happier working abroad. In America, where money was all-important, the competition was destructive. In Europe, life was less stressful and one could live more fully. That the European schools were superior to those in America was another factor to consider. I could have added how much it bothered me that in America people were so spoiled.

Louise and I decided on the date of our marriage: February 6, 1954.

Our religious differences did cause a problem, but only a minor one. Louise's father had been Catholic, and so was I. But Louise was Episcopalian. Monsignor Béla Varga, the exiled president of the Hungarian Parliament, assured me that he could help us. With his connections at the Vatican, he obtained a dispensation for me to marry a Protestant. Today, this problem no longer exists.

After the beautiful ceremony at St. James' (Episcopal) Church, on Madison Avenue at 71st Street, there was a grand reception in Old Westbury at the home of Louise's mother. The only member

My bachelor party just before our wedding

Our marriage

of my family whom Louise had met was my brother, Paul, who was my best man. I think Louise was very brave to marry someone, knowing only one member of his family.

We took a small apartment at 2 Beekman Place and were blissfully happy.

The same year I had a ruptured appendix, and Louise turned out to be an accomplished nurse.

After a while, I was offered the position of assistant district director of American Export Lines in Alexandria, Egypt. Louise and I thought that Egypt would be our home for years, and we were thrilled. I accompanied the party of Grace Kelly to Nice, on her way to wed Prince Rainier of Monaco. We were all traveling on our liner, the *Constitution*. I stayed at Genoa, the European headquarters of our company, for a short time, then proceeded to Piraeus and finally to Alexandria.

With Prince Rainier and Princess Grace of Monaco

Speaking English and with my background, I slipped easily into the routine of my new job.

Egypt and the Suez Crisis, The Hungarian Revolution

I found a wonderful house in Alexandria with a big garden, and with the help of a friend, Louise and I became members of all the best clubs before she even arrived. Taher Pasha, a cousin of the exiled King Farouk, gave us a driver.

In Egypt, there was a very efficient system for running a household: You engaged a head man, called a "sufragi", and he hired whatever staff he thought you would need – cook, gardener, maids, and so on.

Louise flew to Egypt in May 1956 and joined me at Alexandria. Our house was not quite ready, so we rented ex-King Farouk's yacht for a few days. Louise looked lovely and was thrilled by her new surroundings. Every summer, the whole diplomatic community would migrate from Cairo to Alexandria, where there was a lively social life. It was there that we met all the interesting people from the diplomatic corps and the business community. Our house was very comfortable, with plenty of excellent help. Nanny Calder took care of our first child, little Peter (P-1), who looked very handsome with his strikingly blond hair.

Nobody worked in the afternoons. The Automobile Club was for swimming and luncheon, the Sporting Club for tennis and exercise. There were very good Arab horses to ride and in the fall excellent duck shooting in the Nile Delta. The shooting rights for 100,000 acres of delta marshes belonged to the Club de la Chasse et du Pêche. I was lucky enough to get a share in this club for the season.

Prices were very reasonable, compared to those in America. Five household servants cost roughly the same as one in the U.S.A. I liked my work and we were blissfully happy. All this was too good to be true.

It was also too good to last. On July 20, 1956, the dictator of Egypt, Colonel Gamal Abdel Nasser, nationalized the Suez Canal and sank a ship in the waterway to block all traffic, causing an international crisis. The American Embassy sent a letter to all the U.S. citizens in Egypt announcing that it could no longer guarantee their safety. Americans were advised that their wives and children should leave Egypt until the crisis passed. This news hit like a bombshell. No one had expected such an action from Colonel Nasser. What were we to do?

My best friend, Gyuri Ullmann, was by then married to a charming German girl, born Karin Oppenheim. Her family owned Sal. Oppenheim, Jr. & Cie., the largest private bank in Germany. I phoned Gyuri and described our predicament. He said there was no problem: Louise, baby Peter (Gyuri's godson), and our nanny could come and stay with him as long as it was necessary. With a broken heart, I watched my family depart for Cologne. I was again alone. My work, sport, and friends helped to overcome the loneliness, but I missed my family terribly. The rental of our house expired, and the Peels, a leading English family, offered me a house with a garden, free of charge, but I was expected to refurbish it.

By September, the political situation had stabilized, and the U.S. Embassy suggested that family members might return.

You can imagine my joy at having my family back in our new home. We had a great time and went out a lot, but without knowing how long the new peace would last. We became friends with Sir Humphrey and Lady Trevelyan (the British ambassador and his wife), the de Kellers (the Swiss chargé d'affaires and his wife), the Liedekerks (a Belgian diplomatic couple), and others.

Once, when we were house guests at the British Embassy, a lovely building rich in history, Ambassador Trevelyan organized a full-moon riding party. We set out at 10 P.M. from the Great Pyramid and rode through the desert on lovely Arab thoroughbreds to Saqqarah. A big buffet awaited us, and we watched the sun rise.

The next morning, I got a phone call from my assistant in our office at Alexandria with urgent instructions from our New York headquarters. He asked me to write down what he had to say and then read back what I had written. The message was to the effect that we had to be at the port of Alexandria by evening, carrying only hand luggage, and would leave Egypt on the ship *Exocorda*.

I stormed into the British Embassy and told Sir Humphrey about my instructions from New York. He had no news other than that a revolution had broken out in Hungary. I phoned the U.S. Embassy, where a secretary told me that, while shaving, he had heard that the British, French and Israelis had bombed Port

Said. I told him about my message. He said he had no instructions from his superiors.

Louise and I, baby Peter, and Nanny Calder got into our Studebaker station wagon and drove to the port of Alexandria, where we learned more about the revolution in Hungary. It had apparently been organized by the factory workers. The border with Austria was open, there were no guards, and approximately 150,000 Hungarians were fleeing their country.

The *Exocorda* was built for cargo and a maximum of sixty passengers, but there were already three hundred people on board. We asked the captain of the ship what was going on. He told us that war had broken out between Great Britain, France, Israel, and Egypt. The narrow entrance of the port had been closed with a dynamited net. With our binoculars, we could see on the horizon the U.S. Sixth Fleet, which was not at war. The Egyptian harbor master, a shooting friend of mine, told us there was nothing we could do. The government would decide everything. We embraced as he left our vessel. I got a note from him later, when he had become prime minister of Egypt.

The *Exocorda* finally got permission to sail. Our first stop was at Naples, where the U.S. ambassador, Clare Boothe Luce, greeted us. When I asked her for news about the revolution, she told me that Soviet troops had left Hungary, and confirmed that the border with Austria was still open.

When I flew to Vienna to get news of my family, the Order of Malta informed me that thousands of people were walking, night and day, toward the Austrian border, but the Russian Army had returned, and Budapest was now besieged. Some friends told me that the uranium mines in Hungary might be blown up, and they wondered whether this should be done. I was in no position to give them an answer, but I flew to Washington, D.C., and contacted C. D. Jackson, an assistant to President Eisenhower and a former intelligence officer. I met him at the Lloyds' home, and we discussed the uranium mines. When he asked for my opinion, I said that I was an unimportant immigrant and could not advise him. I then asked him what plans the U.S. government had for Hungary. He answered, "No plans," as America was entirely preoccupied with the crisis in Egypt.

I began to travel between Vienna and Washington, helping refugees escape to the West. Louise flew to Vienna, accompanied me to the border, and courageously helped Hungarian refugees from no-man's-land to enter Austria.

Above all, I wanted to bring out my family, but they were not of one mind about leaving Hungary. My father and my brother-in-law were proud and stubborn. "A man does not leave his country!" they insisted. And they had plenty of reasons to leave. Since losing their farms, homes, and all their possessions to the communists, my parents and Irmi's family had been living in two cramped apartments in Budapest. Returning from the concentration camp, my father had found our family crowded into such a tiny space that he had to sleep on the floor.

When Irmi's children tried to escape to Austria, they were arrested at the frontier, beaten up by communist border guards, and turned back. But I refused to be discouraged. I found a former Hungarian army officer who had guided many escapees to freedom and asked him to bring my mother out. I then phoned my cousin Paul Decleva, whose mother was also stuck in Hungary and wanted to leave. We decided to collaborate. Another cousin, Laya de Thassy, decided to join the escape party. In all, there would be eleven fugitives in the group. The guide wanted $2,500 per head. No one knew when the escape would be attempted. Only the guide could decide when the moment was right because it depended on the weather and other variables. My mother had hoped to spend Christmas with her family, but she was suddenly told to be ready to leave on Wednesday December 19, 1956.

The fugitives went to the Western Railway Station in Budapest and joined the guide inconspicuously. One by one, they left the crowd on the platform and walked around to the other side of the train, where there was no one. The engineer helped each person up onto the locomotive and placed him or her in the coal car on top of the coal. They huddled there in the icy darkness for two hours before the train departed, then another two hours crept by before it halted at the Austrian border. There, the usual crowd of communist policemen and customs officials checked people's papers and ransacked the passenger cars for contraband. The locomotive and coal car were uncoupled and parked on a siding. The Austrian locomotive was then coupled on, and the train at last departed for Vienna.

Around 2:00 A.M., the fugitives were told to jump down, one by one, from the abandoned coal car, and with the guide leading, they set out to slip across the border. What lay ahead of them was a desolate no-man's-land riddled with land mines and cleft by a barbed wire fence. There were also watchtowers manned by border guards who would fire illuminating flares into the air and then shoot at whatever moved. Here, at last, was the infamous Iron Curtain, where the hell that Stalin had made suddenly gave way to freedom.

The fugitives drew close as they approached the wire fence. The ground underfoot was furrowed and frozen solid, and it was difficult to walk on. Because there was snow, everyone carried a white sheet to hide under when the guards fired their flares, at intervals of about fifteen minutes. Rifle shots were occasionally heard, but no one was sure who the guards were shooting at.

Using wire cutters, the guide snipped a passage through the fence for the fugitives. More important, he led them safely through the minefield. Still, the escape took several hours and was exhausting. When a flare lit the sky, the fugitives had to drop down suddenly on the rough frozen ground and cover themselves with their sheets. Laya de Thassy, who was 74, passed out and had to be dragged by the others. They nonetheless reached the first Austrian outpost and were welcomed with hot tea, snacks, and beds to sleep on. The next day they were taken to Vienna by bus, but Laya was still unconscious; she did not fully revive for three days.

Louise and I had of course never been told when my mother and her group would attempt to escape. Their guide had chosen the moment on short notice, and complete secrecy had to be maintained. We were in New York when my mother phoned from Vienna and gave us the news. To hear her speaking from a free country was one of the most memorable thrills of my life. In Austria, she was cared for by the Order of Malta. I hurried back to Vienna from New York, where I had been working to get her a visa to enter the U.S.A., the blessed land of freedom. Thanks to Louise, my mother was given a nice apartment in Manhattan.

Among my many friends who escaped from Hungary at this time was Captain Géza Pongrácz, my company commander in the Hussars. Géza, who was somehow related to our colonel, had disappeared at the end of the war and was presumed dead. After a number of years, his wife and daughter were able to obtain a death certificate for him, and the wife proceeded to remarry. She then immigrated to New Jersey with her new husband and with Géza's daughter.

The problem was, Géza wasn't dead. He had simply been taken prisoner, and when the Russians finally released him, he returned to Hungary. After years of suffering in Soviet concentration camps, poor Géza found that his country had been communized, his wife was married to another man, and he himself was officially dead.

In the Revolution of 1956, Géza escaped from Hungary and eventually managed to contact me. We talk about his bizarre predicament for a long time, and I advised him to go to America and try to straighten out the problem with his wife in a civilized way. He asked me to accompany him because my presence might help to diffuse the tension at this surreal meeting. So we journeyed to America and then to New Jersey and eventually found ourselves standing in the presence of Géza's daughter, his wife, and her new husband. There was no "scene". We all agreed to have lunch together, but the tension continued to build as the moment approached when we would have to discuss "the problem". Red wine flowed freely on this extraordinary occasion, and it served its purpose. We all remained civil and even managed to share a few laughs.

When the meal was over, I gently persuaded Géza's wife and daughter to retire to the next room while Géza and I and the second husband attempted to resolve their excruciating dilemma. The wife and daughter were not consulted – Hungary was a man's country in those days.

Red wine continued to flow until the two men and I were quite high. I was deeply moved when the second husband graciously said to Géza, "Of course, you must have your wife back." But Géza slyly replied, "Not so fast. We're not there yet." With Hungarian cunning, the two husbands were bargaining over the wife. They finally made a deal. Géza's wife would remain with her second husband, Géza would take an apartment nearby, and his daughter would stay with either parent whenever she wanted to. It was the kind of civilized agreement that I believe in. Where people behave like gentlemen, lawyers will never be necessary.

When Louise and I returned from Egypt, Mrs. Hitchcock was thrilled to have her daughter back, and Louise had much to relate about her experiences in Egypt and Austria. Meanwhile, American Export Lines had gone broke because the Suez Canal was still blocked, and I was again unemployed.

We rented a very comfortable house in the country, near Westbury, Long Island, and it was then that we met a charming and famous personality, Wernher von Braun. A prodigious inventor, he had headed the German think tank at Peenemünde, where the V-I and V-II guided missiles were invented for Hitler's bombing of Britain. Later, he worked with equal zeal for his former enemies and headed the U.S. National Aeronautics and Space Administration at Huntsville, Alabama. Under his leadership, America landed on the moon.

Paris

My next ambition was to become a stockbroker. I obtained a 93% passing mark on my broker's exam at the Institute of Finance, and Count Hans Czernin, the President of Bache & Company in France, said he would like to have me as his assistant. Hans was the eldest son of the last Austro-Hungarian foreign minister, and in him I found an ideal boss. He liked to shoot and play backgammon, and he put my name down for membership in the Travelers Club. Bache & Company was the second-largest brokerage firm, after Merrill Lynch. Charlie Schwartz, an important partner and close friend of Louise's family, and N.R. Bache gave their blessing, so after a few months working at Bache in New York, Louise and I moved to Paris in February 1959. We stayed for a while in a hotel; then we found a flat at 11 rue Garancière, near the Palais du Luxembourg. Our friend Harry Phipps was also working in the Paris office of Bache, and everything looked very promising.

We eventually left the rue Garancière, when we found a lovely apartment at 54 avenue d'Iéna. The building belonging to Madame Esmond and her sister, Madame de Gunzburg, and the apartment had previously been occupied by Susan Mary Patton, who had been a girlfriend of the British ambassador, Duff Cooper, and was about to marry the journalist Joseph Alsop. Our son Paul (P-2) was born while we were still in New York, but we had room for the two boys and plenty of staff in the new apartment as well as garage space for four cars. I had an ideal situation, but business was slow, and I was allowed to solicit only in France. In London, we were represented by Rupert Löwenstein, and in Italy and Monte Carlo by Dino Pecci Blunt. Our office was at 6 rue Royale, opposite Maxim's restaurant, in what had been the apartment of Madame de Staël. At the end of five years, François Malle, who was on the board of Delafield & Delafield in Paris, took over Lehman Brothers and arranged that I should become the manager of D & D for the whole of Europe. Demi Gates was the foreign partner in New York, and Jackie Pierpont, together with Edward Delafield, then 84 years old, were the sleeping partners. I spoke German perfectly, and Gyuri Ullmann helped me a great deal in Germany. Business was satisfactory, and we had a wonderful time.

We became very friendly with Joyce and Teddy Schultz. Teddy's mother, born Margaret Thompson, was a very wealthy woman whose fortune came from mining and whose second husband, Tony Biddle, had been the U.S. ambassador to Poland. She had two children from her first marriage: Peggy, who married a friend of mine, Alex Hohenlohe, and Teddy, who was badly wounded while landing at Normandy in June 1944. They had houses all over France – in the South, at Fontainebleau, and in Paris. At Benerville-sur-Terre, near Deauville, they had a charming little farm that we would rent. By that time, our Peggy (P-3) had arrived, and we enjoyed some lovely summers at Deauville. Louise would spend the whole summer there with the children, and I would join them on weekends. During the day, there were races, polo, and live pigeon shoots, and in the evenings an active social life, mostly in black tie. For the girls, night life was enlivened by the frequent presence of Porfirio Rubirosa, Élie de Rothschild, and Prince Aly Khan.

Louise liked to ski, and her uncle Matt Mellon had bought a big chalet in Kitzbuehel, Austria, from Count Chappy Seilern. Nearby was a small house, called "Heimchen", which we rented for the Christmas holidays in 1965. Jimmy Van Allen and Michel Carcano were Father Christmas, and Louise made the occasion a real attraction with live donkeys. Family from Pittsburg and friends from New York came to help us celebrate. Louise and the 4 P's – Pauline (P-4) had by then joined the family – all became good skiers. But I broke my leg and decided to leave skiing alone.

In 1969, old Mr. Delafield died, and the firm folded. I knew Donald Stralem, the brother-in-law of Bobby Lehman, and Eddie Lobkowicz, who was already working as a stockbroker in Paris. I got all the loose ends together and we started to work as Stralem & Company, in Eddie's apartment, at 30 avenue Marceau, within walking distance of our flat. Eddie's wife, Françoise, and four lovely children made the atmosphere cheerful.

In the late Sixties, with the help of Philippe de Noailles, we bought a country place at Silly, about an hour from Paris. Louise decorated the house with energy and taste. We had seven hectares and a lake. Ducks and geese, pheasants, a pony, and Hungarian vizsla dogs made the place very amusing for us and, above all, for our children. Yetta and John Goelet, who had a beautiful estate with a swimming pool at the Château of Sandricourt, just twenty minutes away, were more than kind and helpful. Their three wonderful boys became close friends of our children. The Ganay and Mouchy families very kindly invited me to shoot, and so did Robert de Balkany, who had an extraordinary partridge shoot in Spain. These kind and generous friends were out of this world.

My dear mother, who followed us from New York to Paris, got a small apartment in our building. For a moment, everything

Our Family in 1968: (left to right) Paul, Louise, Pauline, myself, Peggy,
and young Peter

looked perfect. But in 1966 my father died, and a few years later
Louise decided to go back to the States with the children. Luckily,
I found a smaller flat in our building, as I did not want to return
to America. The stress would have been too great. I did not grow
up in the U.S.A. and have never been able to relate to fiercely
competitive rich Americans.

One of my first priorities was to find a second source of income.
I decided to put a foot into the shooting world, my true and
holy love.

I remember going to America for Christmas and staying with
my family. Louise was trying her utmost to bring up the 4 P's. She
and her family remained on close terms with me, and I was given
the moral support that I needed to continue my life.

With my sons, Peter (right) and Paul, circa 1970

Finally, I must thank Geneviève Joyot, a lady without whom I would never have been able to live this wonderful and free life. She was a most loyal, intelligent, and sincere friend, helping me all these years, ever since February 1959. Geneviève was at first a secretary. Then she passed the necessary examination and became a registered representative and manager. She eventually became the president of Stralem & Company, our firm. Everyone who knew her respected her.

The Château de la Tour, where I lived for many years in later life

II

Bird Shooting in Old Hungary

I n Hungary, many of us had a passion for shooting. But I really wasn't in Hungary that much, because at the age of sixteen I went to boarding school in Vienna, and between the ages of nineteen and twenty-four I served with my cavalry regiment in the Soviet Union, Poland, Hungary, Croatia, Ruthenia, and Transylvania. I was also preoccupied with studying for my doctorate in political science and for the two Foreign Office exams. Nonetheless, I often found time to walk up some game with dogs or to do some rough shooting.

And during the coldest months, when the temperature can sink to minus 25 Centigrade, I would go out in a sleigh draw by four horses with little bells jingling on them and would feed the game. What fun it was!

If all the property that Hungarian noble families claim to have owned before the communist takeover were heaped together, it would probably amount to more than the whole surface of the earth. So here are some reliable facts. In 1925, the foremost land-owning families in Hungary were:

Esterházy	408,000 acres
Festetics	144,000 acres
Károlyi	114,000 acres
Pallavicini	75,000 acres
Batthyány	65,000 acres
Almásy	45,000 acres
Wenckheim	44,000 acres

The clergy and religious organizations owned an additional 915,000 acres. While none of these properties could compare in size with those of the Polish or Russian noble families, all of them had excellent shoots, which were a source of income to the estates.

Here are some details about what was probably the finest shoot in the world.

Tót-Megyer

In shooting circles, this historic Hungarian estate was not only famous in Central Europe but worldwide. Let me explain why.

Count Lajos ("Luki") Károlyi inherited Tót-Megyer from his father, who had been the Austro-Hungarian ambassador to Britain at the end of the nineteenth century. The estate covered roughly 20,000 acres, and another 20,000 were rented for shooting purposes. These 40,000 acres lay between the rivers Váh and Nyitra, north of the Danube between Budapest and Vienna.

This land had belonged to Hungary until 1920, when the vindictive Treaty of Trianon created an independent Czechoslovakia, and many Hungarian territories became part of Slovakia, with Pozsony (Bratislava or Pressburg) as its capital.

A number of Hungarian kings had been crowned at Pozsony while Buda was under Turkish occupation, in the sixteenth and seventeenth centuries.

At Tót-Megyer, the climate is quite warm. Spring comes early, and the game is born earlier than elsewhere. There are many sugar beet fields, and the insects in those fields are a favourite food for pheasants and partridges.

Count Károlyi did not bother to raise pheasants. All his pheasants were "wild" birds, that is, not hatched by machines or broody hens.

Somebody once asked a rich man, "What is the secret of your being so rich?" He answered, "I spend less than I earn." The same principle applies to managing game. Approximately 30,000 to 40,000 pheasants and partridges remained after the yearly shoots, and these formed the basis of the next year's pheasant and partridge output. But one had to count on occasional severe winters, like the ones in 1928-29 and 1939-40, when half the breeding stock died in spite of daily feeding. For the worst killer of game birds was thick frozen snow at minus 20 to 25 degrees Centigrade.

The second-worst killer was the mowing-up of bird nests. At Tót-Megyer, a way had been found to prevent this. Before the mowing machines moved in to cut the alfalfa and clover fields, which covered 300 to 500 acres each, beaters and keepers would extend a string across the field and hang various noise-making objects on it. This line of noisy devices would be carried down the field. When it approached a nest, the brooding hen pheasant or partridge would fly away. A keeper would then rush up to the abandoned nest and mark its location by driving a stick into the earth beside it. The next day, when the mowers arrived, they would see the sticks and mow around the nests.

The third-worst killer was vermin. And here is the count of predators killed by the keepers at Tót-Megyer between 1930 and 1937:

Foxes	19
Martens	2
Polecats	1,642
Weasels	7,471
Hedgehogs	4,526
Hamsters	8,114
Stray dogs	4,332
Stray cats	7,403
Eagles	8
Falcons and Hawks	174
Buzzards and Merlins	2,742
Magpies	3,223
Crows and Rooks	6,963
Grey-black Crows	4,683
Kestrels	2,787
Different Owls	2,176
Total	55,265

And this was the tally of "noble game" shot at Tót-Megyer between 1930 and 1937:

Roe deer	99
Hares	70,863
Pheasants	75,407
Partridges	80,484
Total	226,853

The best year was 1933:

Hares	11,740
Pheasants	10,723
Partridges	14,989
Rabbits	111
Various	53
Total	37,616

To run such a complex and complicated shoot, you needed first-class devoted personnel. The man who supervised all of the shooting was a highly educated, motivated university graduate. Under him were three head keepers, one for the pheasants, one for the partridges, and one for the hares. Under them were twenty to twenty-five ordinary gamekeepers. On major shooting days, another twenty to twenty-five game personnel were borrowed from the neighboring estates. As each territory was hunted only once a year, this system worked very well.

The shooting personnel had to be paid good wages, but they also needed an incentive. In addition to a nice house and good pay, they would participate in the profits of the shoot. The keepers got fees for the predators they killed and also received generous tips. In other words, a good man had a good job for life, and his sons would too.

You may think that such a professionally run organization earned lots of money. Well, it didn't. Without a yearly kill of 30,000 birds and other game, Tót-Megyer would not even pay for itself.

The greatest expenses were the salaries of the personnel, bonuses for vermin killed, rent for the different shooting rights, and the immense quantity of food needed to ensure that the game would survive the winters. The estate partially offset these expenses by catching live hares, partridges, and pheasants to sell or exchange for other game. Live hares, which were exported to Germany and France, would bring a good price.

Count Károlyi's wife was born Countess Hanna Széchenyi. These two families were related to all of the Hungarian, and to a great part of the Austrian, nobility. But to be invited to shoot at Tót-Megyer, it was not enough to be a relative or close friend of the owner. You had to be an excellent shot and a very correct one, too. Everybody wanted to be invited. *There were too many Eskimos and not enough seals!*

At Tót-Megyer, there were the "regular Guns" – those who would be invited year after year as long as they shot and behaved well. The host did not want to see hares running around on three legs or pheasants with one wing broken. If that happened several times because the Gun was tired or had a bad day, the next year he would be invited to dinner, but not to shoot!

Every Gun had to bring an arsenal of cartridges. In a shoot lasting several days, you would need about 5,000 cartridges per Gun for the pheasants and about 7,000 for the hares. In the castle, there was a special room for the ammunition. Every regular Gun had a wooden box with his name on it. If the host said to one of the Guns, "You can leave some cartridges here," it meant he would be invited back.

Ordinarily, a truck was sent to the best gunsmith in Budapest, from whom all the Guns ordered their cartridges. The gunsmith and an assistant would return with the ammunition in case someone's shotgun malfunctioned. Most of the shooting guests would travel with at least three shotguns, and those who came with "machine guns" (automatics) would have five or six. The automatics were very unpopular, since they were dangerous to reload, but Guns of a certain age or with shoulder problems used them because of their mild recoil.

If you failed to shoot enough birds because one or two of your shotguns broke down, it would certainly count against you. The host and the shooting personnel would work throughout the year to offer you the best flying birds, but they would expect you to hit them. You were there to kill game.

To shoot a large number of birds, you needed excellent loaders with whom you were well co-ordinated. Most Guns arrived with their own loaders, but additional loaders could be obtained from the estate. A loader was not required to watch the game. He had to concentrate entirely on loading the shotguns quickly and safely. Before the shooting season, many guests would train with their personal loaders in a room covered with mattresses or foam rubber. That way, if a valuable shotgun was dropped, no damage was done.

At Tót-Megyer, the summer partridge shoots took place in September and lasted ten to twelve days. Once in a while, the temperature would rise to 30 or 35 degrees Centigrade, so lots of "spritzer" (white wine with soda and ice) and ice-cooled watermelons were consumed. There would be nine or ten Guns divided into two groups. Each group had 60 to 80 beaters. The shoots that were rented from the villages were the best for summer partridges, as they had narrow strips of clover, alfalfa, potatoes, and maize, which the birds frequented. The Guns would normally walk in a single line with the beaters, as in a grouse walk-up. But sometimes the beaters would walk toward the Guns, driving the small strips of ground. Hungarian vizsla dogs were the best for this kind of shooting.

During these shoots in September, between 10,000 and 12,000 partridges would be killed at Tót-Megyer. Count Károlyi's son-in-law once shot more than 1,000 partridges in two days.

For the pheasant drives in November, there would be six or seven Guns and about 400 beaters. On the day before the shoot, the beaters would form a large circle around a 300-acre wooded area. The centre of this circle was called the "pheasant wood". All the pheasants that were out in the fields, reeds, and stubble would walk or fly back into the wood, which was their roosting place or "home". Two hundred beaters would be used for the drives in the wood; the rest would be placed as "stops" around the wood and on the different cuttings ("alleys") in the wood so that the pheasants would not escape from one drive into another. Approximately 100 beaters would be used in each drive, and 100 more would be lined up for the next drive, to save time. After every drive, the Guns would walk, or would be driven in horse-drawn carriages, to the next location, where an additional 100 beaters would be ready and waiting. The initial 100 beaters would line up for the third drive, while the second drive was in progress.

A line of gamekeepers with perfectly trained dogs made the "pick up", laying the dead birds in the "alleys", where heavy ox-drawn wagons were waiting to collect them.

Only with such detailed and precise organization was the host able to have twenty-four drives per day, twelve before the very simple luncheon, which lasted only twenty minutes, and twelve more afterwards. As a rule, no alcohol was served at the short midday meal, but in very cold weather a glass of hot red wine would be permitted. The fare consisted of a hot soup and one dish, served around big open fires. In mid-November, we could shoot only until 4:30 P.M., so the whole hunt had to be timed with military precision.

A few days before every shoot, there would be rehearsal drives, with no shooting permitted. The pheasants would be driven just as they would be in the drives that were to come. They were being trained to fly correctly! Though they were not compelled to fly very high, in those rather low woods, they were wild birds, not released, and they flew quite well. The Guns were expected not to shoot the very low birds, and the host kept watch to make sure that no one did. To shoot a low bird counted against you.

At Tót-Megyer there would be twenty-four drives in a day, and with eight Guns shooting, the bag per drive would come to perhaps 160 cock pheasants or 20 cocks per Gun. The daily total would therefore amount to between 3000 and 4000 cock pheasants.

There was an extraordinary year – 1909 – when the hatching and climatic conditions had been so outstanding that the host decided to try for an all-time record bag. He allowed hen pheasants to be shot in every second drive. The Guns were:

> Count Lajos Károlyi (the host)
> Count Béla Széchenyi (the host's father-in-law)
> Count Magi Apponyi
> Count Ivan Draskovich
> Count Rudolf Erdödy
> Count László Hunyady (later killed by a lion)
> Count Karl Schönborn
> Baron Jozsi Inkey

The conditions were perfect: an incredible abundance of pheasants, a number of fabulous shots, no sun, no wind, and dry weather. The daily bag came to 6,125 pheasants and 223 partridges and hares – a total of 6,448 "noble game". In *The Big Shots*, on page 134, J. G. Ruffer states that the Tót-Megyer shoot of December 10, 1909 is still a world record. Three Guns shot over a thousand pheasants each, that day, and Count Draskovich, with a bag of 1,212, shot the most.

I must now describe the field drives at Tót-Megyer in December that would last a week. Imagine a large parallelogram or brick-shaped area, with the long sides, or flanks, four to six kilometers long. Eight to ten Guns would be lined up on one of the short sides of the parallelogram, with 20 beaters between each Gun. In a field drive, three consecutive lines, including Guns, beaters, keepers, coat porters, and picker-ups would advance toward a line of keepers and beaters standing motionless, like a backstop, at the far end of the driven area.

The opposing line:
At the far end of the driven area stood a line of 200 men,
with one keeper between every 10 beaters.
This line was to block the birds from escaping
and to drive them back toward the advancing Guns,
at the conclusion of the drive.

▲
Direction
of the
Drive

The Area To Be Driven
(often several kilometers long)

▲
Direction
of the
Drive

First line, moving forward:
Eight to 10 Guns, with 20 beaters between each Gun
and one keeper between every 10 beaters,
about 200 men in all, with the host, his horn-blower,
and his messengers, all on horseback, at the center of the line.

Second line, moving forward:
The loaders and cartridge bearers,
coat porters, and picker-ups who retrieved the birds and hares.

Following at the end:
A number of wagons to carry the dead game,
each drawn by four to six oxen.

At a signal from the host, the horn-blower would sound the advance, and the line of Guns would start to move across the

Grouse

Cock pheasant

Hare

fields. On a frosty day, to walk was quite easy, but when it was wet, every Gun lifted two to five pounds of mud with every step, and the drives would average four to six kilometers in length.

On both flanks, the beaters would wave their arms to prevent the birds from escaping to the sides. The host had five or six messengers on horseback and the horn-blower at his side, and the different horn signals – stop, move faster, go slower, etc. – were instantly obeyed by the gamekeepers and beaters of the estate and by those that had been borrowed from the neighboring shoots. If there was fog or rain, the problems could be formidable.

Once the drive started to move forward, most of the game would run or fly away from the Guns. The farther the birds were driven, the more they wanted to return to their "home", i.e. backward, toward the Guns. The line of advancing beaters and Guns would be clearly visible to the birds because the land was completely flat. In December, the birds would rise up well in front of the line of Guns, and that made for difficult, excellent shooting. About half a mile from the end of the drive, the opposing line of beaters, which had been waiting at the far end of the parallelogram, would begin to move forward toward the advancing line of Guns. As the two lines moved toward one another, the Guns would stop briefly to prepare themselves for the last and best half hour of the day, the climatic "back drive". The opposing lines would then continue to walk very slowly toward one another. There would be thousands of birds between them. Hundreds of pheasants would be rising and hares scooting about. The back drive would yield about 1,000 cock pheasants, 500 to 600 partridges, and 400 to 500 hares. The record for partridges shot by one Gun in a back drive was 118.

Behind each Gun would be two loaders, two cartridge bearers, one coat bearer, two pairs of lads to pick up and carry the pheasants, another pair for the partridges, and two more pairs for the hares.

The dead birds and hares would be left on the dirt roads, where the keepers would make the count and draw up a detailed summary of the day's kill. The game would then be piled into the ox wagons that trailed along behind the Guns. Every animal would be gutted, and those that were not eaten locally would be exported by rail to Germany or France.

Tót-Megyer was indeed unique!

Pusztaszer

Owned by the Marquis Alfons Pallavicini, Pusztaszer was considered the second-best shoot in Hungary. It was also the place where the pagan Magyar tribes had elected Arpád as their ruler. His family reigned from approximately 900 until 1310. This dynasty gave Christianity five saints and was very prosperous.

Here are some details about the shoot at Pusztaszer, on December 4, 1930.

The schedule:	Breakfast at 7 A.M.
	Departure at 7:30 A.M.
	Beginning of the shoot at 8 A.M.
The Guns:	Count Zsiga Batthyány
	Count József Cziráky
	Count Pál Draskovich
	Count Ferenc Erdödy
	Count Imre Hunyady
	Count Alexander Pallavicini
	Count Alfons Pallavicini
	Prince Adolf zu Schwarzenberg
	Count Stefan Széchenyi
	Count Hubert Voykffy
The beaters:	500
The transport:	For the guests: 5 carriages, four in hand, and 5 two-horse carriages
	For the police: 2 two-horse carriages
	For the game: 12 carriages, each drawn by 4 oxen, and 12 additional carriages, each drawn by 2 oxen

At the end of the day, in front of the Château of Pusztaszer lay 5,074 "noble game" animals: pheasants, partridges and hares.

About Pheasants

In ancient Greek times, pheasants were found in the land known as Kolchis, between the Caspian and Black seas. Today, this region is known as Georgia (Gruzia).

The Latin name for the original pheasant is *phasianus colchicus*. It is a beautiful long-tailed bird with a green head, but it lacks the white ring around the neck that some other pheasants have. In German, it is called *fasan*, in French *faisan*, in Italian *fagiano*, in Portuguese *faisao*, and in Hungarian *facan*.

In the Middle Ages, we find pheasants in the British Isles, probably introduced by the Romans during their occupation, which lasted several hundred years. In the eleventh century, we hear of pheasants in the Czech kingdom.

Pheasant shoots began to appear with the invention of "modern" shotguns in the eighteenth century. At that time, the best-known shoot was the one organised in Bohemia by Prince Colloredo for Emperor Francis I. It lasted eighteen days and 116,209 shots were fired. The guns were muzzle-loaded, so everyone came with eight to ten guns. The bag totalled 47,950 pieces, of which 9,500 were pheasants.

On November 24, 1796, seven Guns shot 1,200 pheasants at Freienberg, one of Prince Schwarzenberg's estates. Lord Malmesbury, who witnessed one of these early bird shoots, reports that the Guns were placed twenty to twenty-five yards apart, that each hunter came with seven or eight muzzle-loading shotguns, and that the pheasants flew very poorly.

After the Crimean War (1854-56), the English gentry retired to their country estates to enjoy the peace. Today's practice of breeding and shooting pheasants that would be "sporting birds" began at about that time. Big kills became common in Central Europe at the end of the nineteenth century, and the shooting of difficult, high-flying birds became popular between the two world wars.

Besides the *phasianus colchicus*, we have the smaller, better-flying *phasianus torquatus*, which has silvery wings and a telltale white ring around its neck.

From Japan, we have the *phasianus versicolor*, the green or Japanese pheasant, the smallest species. It tends not to run before the beaters and generally takes off rapidly. The hen is quite dark, and many Guns confuse it with the cock bird. It is a shy breeder and does not do well in cold winters.

There are, as you know, many other types of pheasants, among them the golden, silver, king, Reeve, and Lady Amherst. In certain places there are king pheasant drives. It is easy to miss these birds on account of their long tail feathers.

The Two Kinds of Shots

Outstanding shots fall into two categories, the predictable and the unpredictable.

The predictable shot is always at his best, produces in sunshine or rain, and never disappoints his host. He functions like a machine!

The unpredictable shot is full of nerves, much more colorful, and more variable. Should he have slept badly, he will miss several pheasants in a row. On the other hand, he is faster and kills birds that the predictable shot would not have dared to shoot at, fearing to miss them and damage his reputation. He is like an erratic genius. He can shoot with any gun, at any height, faster than anybody, *provided* he is "turned on". And with these qualities, he is always more popular than the predictable shot.

As a rule, any outstanding shot is relaxed, simple, natural, and never in a hurry. If you watch him from a distance, even the most difficult birds appear easy to kill. He chats continuously with a lady companion while shooting a bird with his right barrel and another with his left. He can laugh at a joke while shooting the highest birds.

Some Pointers on Shooting

I believe that one should shoot with friends – with a group of like-minded people whose company you will enjoy all day and all evening. Nowadays, there are almost only commercial shoots left, where you belong to a syndicate or rent a few days' shooting. That's a great pity. The best private shoots were better managed and more enjoyable. People who have to pay for their shooting want the best for their money. They want ever more and better birds. But the modern commercial shoots leave many Guns dissatisfied.

As to the need for practice in bird shooting, many people say, "Of course, you're still a good shot! One never forgets how to shoot well. It's just like swimming, cycling, or ice skating." Frankly, I don't agree. You need to stay in practice. You must shoot quite a few cartridges a year to stay in really top form.

If you lose your self-confidence by shooting infrequently, you become less steady, more uncertain, and less accurate in judging distances. You miss birds that you could not possibly have missed before. Naturally, with time, your eyes don't function so well. Once you need spectacles, it diminishes your accuracy, especially in the rain. You slow down. You can still remain a very good shot, but probably not as good as before.

Bird shooting is a formal sport governed by strict rules, and here are some pointers to bear in mind.

Always kill wounded birds, but don't shoot birds that have passed behind you unless they are wounded.

Don't shoot low birds. It is not sporting to turn a bird that flies near you into "hamburger", with feathers flying in all directions. Such birds are inedible and impossible to sell.

Shoot the birds as far in front of you as you can. A bird flying toward you at 25 miles an hour is on top of you very quickly! And remember that when you shoot an approaching bird, the pellets meet the bird head-on and have a greater penetrating force. Conversely, when a bird is flying rapidly away from you, the pellets have to overtake the bird, as both are travelling in the same direction. The striking power is therefore only half as great as it would be if the bird were flying toward you.

You will often have problems with birds "curling". You can see how much they are curling by raising the barrels of your gun toward an oncoming bird. Often you will see that the bird is actually not coming straight toward you but is curving (curling) steadily to the right or left.

Birds are alarmed by human voices. You should be silent before and during the drive. Don't slam the doors of vehicles. Beaters should not shout unless the drive goes against the wind and the birds are tending to fly back over their heads. Normally, the beaters should clap their hands and slap their sticks.

People who shoot over-and-under guns, which have become increasingly popular, have the arguable advantage of looking along a single barrel instead of two. But the loading of over-and-under guns is more difficult because putting the cartridge in the lower barrel takes more time if you don't open the gun correctly. That's why people don't like to use these guns when the shooting is heavy and fast.

For safety reasons, automatic guns are not allowed on most European shoots. After firing a shot, it is difficult to put the safety catch on quickly while giving the gun to your loader. Automatics are very good if you are shooting alone, sitting in a duck blind, or shooting pigeons or doves. The ones that are gas-operated have

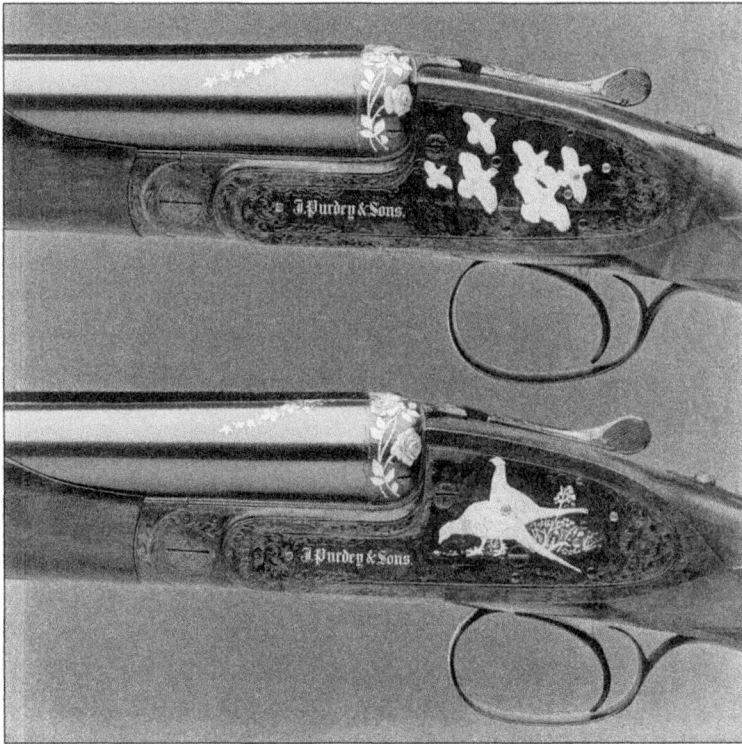

A vulgar, loudly-engraved pair of Purdeys

almost no recoil. But don't use the fifth cartridge. Leave it in the barrel; otherwise you waste time when reloading.

While we are on the subject of guns, if you are young, really keen on bird hunting, and have many years of shooting ahead of you, buy a "trio" – three guns. If you can afford it, buy English guns, new or second hand. The best ones are good investments.

Purdey, Holland & Holland, Boss, and Woodward are the finest English shotguns. Atkins, Lang, Churchill, Grant, Rigby, and Dickson are also very good.

If you can't afford English guns, get yourself a trio of Spanish guns, which are good, reliable, and well priced. Garby, Arietta, Arisabelaga, and Aya are the best names. You can pick the wood for the stock, but don't have the action engraved with a portrait of

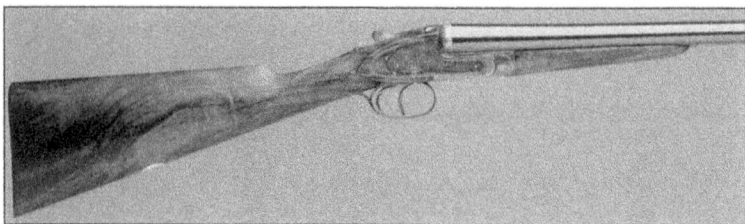

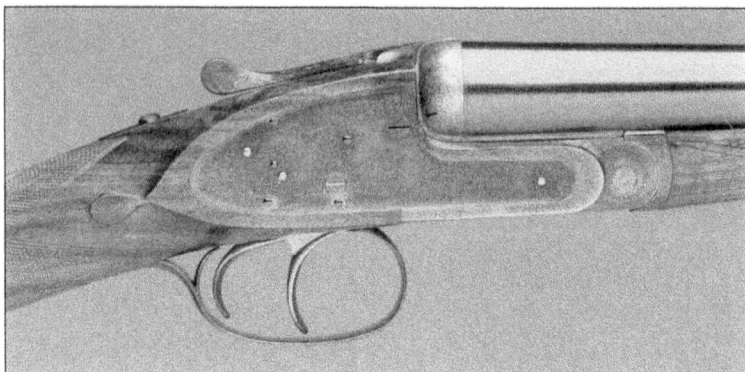

A modest tastefully-engraved Purdey

your labrador or a flying game bird. Such engravings are entirely cosmetic, very expensive, and are viewed as *nouveau riche.*

There are also some good German and Belgian guns. But remember that while a Ford is a very good car that takes you everywhere, a Rolls-Royce, Mercedes, or BMW is a different cup of tea.

Shoot everything with the same guns, from clay pigeons to snipe. That way you will get to know your guns intimately.

A popular rule of thumb is to shoot partridges and grouse with unchoked 26-inch barrels, ducks and geese with 30-inch full-choked barrels, and pheasants with 28-inch barrels choked down to modified. But remember that the main objective should always be to hit the bird in the head or neck. A very high sporting bird that is struck only in the body will usually escape wounded. You should therefore aim so that the head and neck of your bird are placed in the center of your pattern of pellets. And be sure to

Properly attired, the Duke of Westminster shooting grouse at Abbeystead

shoot with barrels that have enough choke. If your pattern is too thin, the bird's head and neck, which are very small targets, may pass between the pellets, even if you are aiming perfectly.

Twenty-gauge guns give you great satisfaction. You can shoot with them just as far as with a 12-bore. But don't shoot with a 410, as you will wound lots of birds. And don't shoot heavily loaded cartridges, as they don't pattern well and are not necessary. They are also bad for your barrels, your head, and your shoulder. The maximum load should contain 32 grams, or one and one sixteenth ounces, of powder.

You must use gun slings. I prefer the simple canvas ones with leather reinforcements, as they dry well and quickly. The fancy leather ones lined with sheepskin may feel more comfortable, but once they get really wet, it takes hours to dry them out. Never put your guns in wet or damp slipcovers overnight, as they will get rusty. And don't put leather objects – shoes, cartridge bags, etc. – close to the fire, or they will be ruined.

Use rubber boots only if you really need them. Get yourself two good pairs of hunting shoes from a good boot maker, also a pair of ankle boots, which will make it easier for you to climb. Don't try to economize on footwear. Get the best and then take care of it. Use shoe trees and polish your boots well every time you wear them. They should last forever.

A Barbour-like overcoat and trousers are a must in your wardrobe. You can put them into a small bag with an extra pullover, gloves, camera, and medicine kit.

Don't dress up in rubber from head to foot on a beautiful day. It looks ridiculous and isn't necessary.

You get dressed to go to a dinner party, a wedding, a cocktail party, etc. Likewise, if you shoot regularly, get yourself two good shooting suits, which will last for years. Order two pairs of trousers, as they'll wear out quicker than your jacket. A tweed suit with breeches, plus fours or walking breeches, are also basic requirements.

You need warm, windproof, waterproof gear. The secret of keeping warm is to wear several thin layers of clothing: silk undershirt and longjohns, both in thermal wear, a wool or cashmere pullover, and so on. Too much thick clothing will keep you from moving freely.

You can often shoot without a regular jacket – in a sleeveless jacket or jersey, both of which are very comfortable. But have a small bag on hand with an extra pullover, gloves, your rain gear, camera, and medicine kit.

Shooting sticks are all right. They consist of a long shepherd's crook on which to lean and a tripod seat measured to your height.

Wear no emblems on your cap or hat except perhaps that of your host. You can see people with hats that have twenty or thirty emblems on them, even feathers sticking out. And don't wear any leather that looks new, whether it be your shoes, cartridge bag, or gun sling. Polish it and give it a worn look beforehand. New leather marks you as a newcomer to the sport. It also suggests new money.

Nowadays, on many shoots there are too many Guns, so they stand too close to one another. I am sure you know the saying "Better a pheasant missed than a pheasant shared." In Spain, the competition is often extreme. A duchess can jump out from her stand like a tigress to pick up one of *your* birds. Let her do it. Someone else's tasteless behavior is no excuse for you to lower your standards.

In our commercial world, the cost of shooting is less per capita with more Guns. But if you invite a large number of friends, don't hesitate to put them in two lines – several Guns in front and the rest behind. When there are not enough pheasants, ask the first row to shoot only cock birds.

If possible, avoid shooting pheasants in the woods. Get them out of their habitat or "home", then drive them back or "homewards", placing the Guns in their flight path. Don't hesitate to put a few beaters with flags in front of the line of Guns. Once the pheasants decide to fly "home", flag waving will not make them change course, but it should make them fly higher. If there is a strong headwind, you might as well change the direction of the drive, because a headwind will turn the pheasants back or out of the drive. Pheasants should be driven with the wind and, if possible, never against the sun.

When pheasants reach their top speed, they don't move their wings any more; they just keep them open and glide, or "plane". These "planers" are the fastest birds, though they don't look like it. You must swing far ahead of them, whether they are flying at angles or toward you.

You can shoot for as long as you like, but I suggest that you shoot only as long as you enjoy it and as long as you are safe and do not spoil other people's fun.

Loaders keep their heads down as King Edward VII blazes away at pheasants on his Sandringham estate.

Loaders

If you are shooting with two shotguns and need a loader, make sure that safety comes first. Guns get excited. They try to shoot too fast if many birds are flying, and they forget to put on the safety catch as they pass the gun to the loader, whether they have fired one shot or two. The loader may never have loaded before, so have a nice chat with him before the first drive. Remember that in a shoot you may survive being peppered with shot by your neighbor Gun, but if you have an accident with your loader, it can easily be fatal because he is so near.

In Spain, after a big luncheon, where the Guns have spiked their coffee with *chinchón* and the loaders have done likewise, shooting can become very dangerous. I shot once with four men, all one-eyed due to shooting accidents.

Load your gun only after you reach your stand and the drive has begun. When it ends, unload your gun immediately. Look through the barrels before you help pick up the birds you have shot. Remember that the barrels of your gun should always be pointing toward the ground or into the air. When loading, point the barrels toward the ground and raise the lock.

Your cartridge bag should have a wide opening, so your loader can get his hand in easily. And don't wear a cartridge belt on a driven shoot, even if you are shooting with only one gun.

If you are fit enough and your loader is an elderly man, give him a hand and carry one of your guns, your coat, and shooting stick. He will be grateful and you will be popular.

Waiting for the birds

III

A Hunter's Story

Having briefly sketched for you the main events of my life, I would now like to record my hunting and shooting experiences because they gave me so much pleasure and occupied so much of my time.

I must now thank my dearest friends who were kind enough to invite me for those lovely days. I will see you all in the eternal shooting grounds, where we will be united forever – hopefully.

The Ganay Family

One could write a long book about this lovely family, which is unique not only in France but anywhere.

The five Ganay brothers had the most charming parents, Rosita Bemberg, from Argentina, and the Marquis Hubert de Ganay, a very handsome gentleman and an excellent sportsman. Their two châteaus, Courances and Fleury, about sixty kilometers from Paris, were not only beautiful but cozy and usually full of family members, which gave them a warm atmosphere.

When Louise and I moved to Paris in February 1959, Hubert de Ganay kindly invited me to shoot pheasants and gray partridges at Courances. I remember that on the first drive, he did not shoot but stood watching me. I think he wanted to take a close look at this Hungarian who had been recommended to him by his cousin Teddy Bemberg, the president of the Rheingold brewery in New York and a friend of ours. I was quite nervous, as I hadn't shot sporting pheasants for many years. At the beginning of the first drive, a high-flying hen pheasant flew toward me while the other Guns were still loading up. I hit this high bird and brought it down. I was very proud and looked with one eye to Hubert, hoping for some sign of appreciation. But he just said, "Peter, please shoot the birds in the head, not in the wing." I was desperate and wanted to disappear. But at the end of the drive, Hubert said, "You did not shoot badly after all." My confidence returned.

Jean-Louis

The eldest son and present marquis, Jean-Louis, is a war hero and also a hero of the French Resistance during World War II. On two occasions, he parachuted into France from England. He and his wife, the former Philippine de Noailles, are a charming couple and very popular all over the world.

Jean-Louis has two great loves, Philippine and Courances, the château where they mainly live. They have three lovely daughters, and their husbands also added greatly to this very special family.

Hubert and Rosita de Ganay rebuilt and divided the neighboring château of Fleury into three parts for their second, third, and fourth sons, André, Michel, and Charles. Their fifth son, Paul, received yet another château, behind Courances, so the members of this family live very close to one another.

Courances, principle château of the Ganay family

André

The second son, André, married a very attractive Argentine girl, and they lived in her country. André became president of Quilmes, the well-known brewery of the Bemberg-Ganay family. His specialty was grouse shooting in Scotland. He shot every year at Invermark and with Lord Cowdray. He later became an accomplished breeder of racehorses in Argentina.

Michel

The third son, Michel, raised cattle in Argentina and was producing milk and cheese. He married a nearly "too beautiful" girl, Victoire. They had three charming and talented sons, Pierre, François, and Sebastian – one nicer and more fun than the other. Sebastian is an internationally recognized painter: his arresting group portrait of the five Ganay brothers hangs in the billiard

The brothers Ganay (left to right seated) André, Paul, and Jean-Louis, (standing) Charles (left) and Michael

room at Courances. Field Marshal Montgomery gave the Ganays the billiard table after World War II as thanks for his stay in their château.

Michel is an accomplished photographer and has organized his delightful pictures into a number of intriguing albums. It would be hard to find a nicer or more generous person than Michel.

Charles

The fourth son, Charles, has a very special sense of humor. He graduated from Harvard University, where he was president of the Porcellian Club. He was also secretary and president of the French Retrievers Club. I shot for this club occasionally and Élie de Rothschild, who was interested in this organization, once told me: "Peter, please wing-shoot a lot of pheasants so that I can see how these dogs work on wounded birds."

Charles was also president of the International Falconry Society. At one point, the Comité International de la Chasse had a falconry department. Some people were breeding falcons in captivity from eggs that had been stolen in North Africa. There was quite a black market in falcons at that time because many Middle Eastern sheiks and emirs were paying insanely high prices for them. Charles handled this problem with a strong hand but also with great diplomacy.

Sheik Zayed of Abu Dhabi was probably the most famous falconer of his day, but I think that Charles de Ganay's knowledge of falconry, which is said to be one of the oldest sports, was more diversified and more thorough.

At Courances, a wild boar hunt took place in a game park of about 400 acres. Charles was in charge of this hunt, and Jean-Louis would walk with the beaters. We were placed in *miradors* (elevated blinds) for safety. The hunt was beautifully organized. I always got very excited and would have difficulty hitting the running pigs with my 9.3 x 64 express rifle.

It is dangerous to shoot with rifles, but during the 30 to 35 years that I attended this shoot yearly, there was never an accident, due to the perfect organization. The largest number of boars killed in a day was 86, taken by twelve to fourteen Guns, during a shoot given for the Count of Barcelona, father of the present King of Spain.

Paul

The fifth son, Paul, was the financial representative of the family and was in contact with the most successful bankers and money managers. He also organized the family's pheasant, Spanish partridge, and grouse shoots. There were enough Ganays and Bembergs to make a line of eight guns, or twelve, when in Spain. I was very lucky to be invited on some of these shoots, and I enjoyed them enormously. Paul, who recently died, was a lifelong friend of mine. His wisdom, kindness, and loyalty will be missed by everyone who had the pleasure of knowing him.

John and Yetta Goelet

The estate named Sandricourt was bought by the elder Robert Goelet before World War I. It covered about 10,000 hectares and was one of the largest properties in France. I remember that an English keeper, ironically named Loader, came with the property and died there, at over 90 years old.

Mr. Goelet, Sr. was chairman of the family-controlled Chemical Bank and Trust Company (of New York). He was also a fine sportsman and developed Sandricourt until it was one of the leading pheasant and partridge shoots in Europe.

When Louise and I moved to Paris, old Mr. Goelet's younger son, John, was in charge of Sandricourt. He had married a charming Anglo-Danish lady named Yetta, and he was temporarily serving as a U.S. soldier in Germany. Sandricourt was rented by Alain and Élie de Rothschild, and Gyuri Nemes, an old Hungarian friend of mine, was in charge of the shoot.

At Sandricourt there was a famous drive called Grand Val. It took place in a valley, deep and wide, where we would do four drives back and forth. We called this strategy "Flick-Flock". High up on one side of the valley was a fence, behind which there were fields of maize, alfalfa, and other crops that pheasants like. When the birds were driven against the fence and took flight, they had to fly across the valley to where eight or ten Guns would be waiting. After each drive, the Guns would turn around, and the next drive would come from the opposite direction. In these four drives we would shoot about 300 to 500 very high sporting birds. Mr. Loader, the head keeper, ran the shoot extremely well. When John Goelet left the army and settled at Sandricourt, he continued to shoot the Grand Val. It was the greatest Christmas present to be invited there, as this drive was probably the best in Europe – this, or the drive known as Grand Goulet, which was also at Sandricourt.

Close by was a lovely *rendezvous de chasse* in an ancient little château named Saint Lubin. An enormous stuffed brown bear was kept there, and it was always a great attraction for our children. Next to the château stands a lovely 800-year-old church, which dates from the time of the Teutonic Order, and is connected to Sandricourt by a tunnel. Only God knows what is in that tunnel.

A perfectionist, John Goelet created new drives, including one near Méru, which yielded hundreds of grey partridges. It would be hard to find more generous hosts than John and Yetta, who is a *grande dame* with rare qualities. One year, they were kind enough to give me Sandricourt for two days of shooting. I rented the hotel in nearby l'Isle-Adam, a charming village. Among my guests were the U.S. ambassador, David Bruce, some Wittgensteins and Ganays, the Duke of Mouchy, Gyuri Ullmann, and Robert de Balkany. I remember that we ate foie gras and woodcock, a Hungarian dish, with magnums of Château Lafitte, a present from Gyuri Nemes. There was a Hungarian Gypsy band and a hairdresser for the ladies. John thoroughly enjoyed himself and gave me two very amusing paintings that still hang above my bed. I think of Sandricourt and the Goelets every day.

Yetta and John had three beautifully brought-up boys: Philip, a scientist, Christopher, a geologist and businessman, and Thomas, who left us, tragically, in his youth. They were educated at Eton, Cambridge, and Oxford – just look at them and you see it. These boys became close friends of our children, and we were always welcome at their pool and tennis court.

John would shoot grouse at Invermark, in Scotland, and he rented from Stagni Urquijo a fine red-legged partridge shoot in Spain, named Frenedas Altas, where Didi Kesselstatt, the Ganays, and Peter Salm were regular Guns.

As time passed, John became more interested in projects on three or four continents. With his great energy and brilliant mind, he became an accomplished businessman and developed an interest in international politics.

God bless the Goelets!

Robert de Balkany

In the early 1960s, Robert de Balkany rented the estate in Spain known as Casarubios del Monte through the Duke of Arión, who helped him to organize a partridge shoot there. But first I must introduce Robert, who is in every way an extraordinary man – brilliant in business and a wonderful friend.

Robert's family came from Transylvania, which had belonged to Hungary for a thousand years but was ceded to Romania in 1920. Almost three million unwilling Hungarians were forced to become Romanians. And that created a problem that continued up through World War II.

Robert's father, Aladár, was also a brilliant businessman. During World War II he left Romania, bought the lovely Château of Saint-Mesme, 45 kilometers from Paris, and settled there. The château had belonged to the brothers Saint, who had set aside about 700 hectares for shooting.

Robert speaks perfect Hungarian, English, French, Italian, and Spanish. He and his father bought some land near Versailles and built the Parly II shopping center. An immediate success, Parly II continued to grow until it became the most important

Saint-Mesme, château of Robert de Balkany

With my lifelong friend Robert de Balkany at his château, Saint-Mesme

project of its kind in Europe – so much so that the Soviet Union sent a planeload of technicians to study it.

The Balkanys bought the best house on the Côte d'Azur, possibly the best private palace in Paris, on the rue de Varennes, and rented – luckily for us – Casarubios del Monte. I don't remember how many shooting days Robert had there, but luckily I was invited to this fabulous shoot every year.

In Spain, there are usually more Guns in a shoot than in England. Twelve or fourteen would be normal. Gonzalo Arión helped Robert arrange the shooting, and the head keeper, Luís, who was always on horseback, conducted the drives professionally and with an iron hand. Every Gun and his loader got a *coto de caza*, which indicated his next position in the line of Guns. I

Yours Truly   Hansi Hohenzollern

still have a card with the names of the Guns and the results for December 17, 1966.

Robert must have rented Casarubios for about fifteen years, and it became one of the finest and most enjoyable shoots in Spain. Many names from the Almanac of Gotha were shooting there, as well as a large number of financiers. More important, Robert had a talent for inviting people who enjoyed not only the quality and quantity of the birds but also the company, which is just as important or even more so.

What a difference it makes to shoot with invited friends instead of unknown paying guests! That all the Guns knew one another and were old friends is what made shooting with Robert so special.

Ferdinand Bismarck   Moritz von Hessen

The Stirling Family

As I mentioned earlier, in 1946 and '47 I had an English friend in Budapest, Peter Stirling. A career diplomat, he had served in Cairo under Field Marshal Montgomery during World War II and was then appointed as a political officer in the British section of the Allied Control Commission for Hungary. Peter was a fine shot and an excellent horseman. He also liked girls and whisky.

In England and Scotland, it was customary for a landed estate to be inherited by the eldest son, thus keeping the fortune in the family. The girls and younger sons would be given a good education and not much else.

As the second son, Peter Stirling joined the British Foreign Office, and after retiring, established himself in Teheran, Iran, where there was good living, while the Pahlavi dynasty lasted. Peter later introduced me to a half-brother of the last shah, Prince Abdorreza, who remained a friend of mine until his early death in 2004.

In the winter, Prince Abdorreza lived in Palm Beach, Florida. He and I shot bobwhite quail there over dogs. We also took part in a "tower shoot" for pheasants. To a European, this kind of shooting is revolting. In America, it is viewed as the way to shoot high birds. The prince was an accomplished rifle shot, and he had the finest collection of big game trophies in the world.

Peter called me one day to say that his elder brother, Lieutenant-Colonel William Stirling, who owned 70,000 acres in Perthshire, Scotland, would like to meet me. We had lunch in London, and Bill told me that he wanted to start commercial shooting on his property. After studying the situation for a few days at Bill's country seat, which was just opposite historic Stirling Castle, I accepted his proposal to provide enough paying guests to make his shoot profitable.

Bill was the son of Brigadier Archibald Stirling of Keir and Cowder. The family's 2,000-acre estate on the outskirts of Glasgow had unfortunately been sold too early and had become part of the expanding city. Today, it would be worth a colossal

Col. Bill Stirling (left) with Count François de Riocour

fortune. Bill was born in 1911, graduated from Ampleforth, and then from Trinity College, Cambridge. He served in the Scots Guards from 1932 to '36.

Bill's younger brother, Lieutenant-Colonel David Stirling, had founded the Special Air Services during World War II. In a series of daring raids, he had proven the value of the SAS to General Sir Claude Auchinleck, the commander of British forces in the Mediterranean, but he was eventually captured and imprisoned in the Colmnitz concentration camp. Bill Stirling, meanwhile, fought with distinction in Tunisia and Sicily. When the Allies landed at Normandy in June 1944, he objected to a plan for dropping his regiment between the German armored infantry and its armored reserves, and resigned his command.

In business, Bill didn't have much luck. He lost 4,000 acres of good farmland on Mount Kilimanjaro, in Tanzania, to President Julius Nyerere's policy of "Africanization". He nonetheless became friends with President Jomo Kenyatta of Kenya, having taken the trouble to visit the African leader when he was still in jail. Bill eventually sold his Perthshire estate, Keir, to an Arab syndicate headed by the ambassador to Britain of the United Arab Emirates, Mohammed Altajer. A clause in the contract permitted the Arabs to take possession of Castle Keir after giving one year's notice. Bill's beautiful wife, Suzie, moved into Keir and announced that if an Arab tried to enter, she would shoot him. She was evicted by court order.

One day Bill's daughter, Hannah, the Marchioness of Salisbury, was expecting a visit from her father at Hatfield Castle. When Bill failed to show up for twenty-four hours, the family broke into his Park Lane apartment in London and found him unconscious, with a broken leg and broken fingers. He died in King Edward VII Hospital for British officers.

We cut the number of gamekeepers at Keir from sixteen to eight. In finding jobs for those who had to be dismissed, Bill's cousin Lord Lovat and his broth-in-law Lord Dalhousie were helpful. Bill had taken two of his gamekeepers with him to the SAS, saying, "I want to see some friendly faces."

At Keir, we eventually raised 30,000 pheasants, which would be released in July. Shooting would begin on November 15th, which allowed enough time for the pheasants to become strong birds.

When Bill lost Keir Castle, we arranged to lodge our shooting parties at Ochtertyre House, which belonged to a helpful Dutch couple, Dick and Windy Groot. And when Dick sold Ochtertyre, we resorted to Cromlix House, a well-run hotel that belonged to the Hon. Ronnie Eden.

The best Guns were given the drives with the high-flying pheasants. Americans and other bad shots got the slower, lower birds. We also had to work out which room each guest should occupy and what arrangements should be made for dinner. Lunch was always eaten in the field and without hard liquor. Luckily, we found a good cook and assistant.

Glen Eagles was only twenty minutes away, and since shooting is not permitted in Britain on Sundays, we would take our guests to "G.E.", with its three world-class golf courses.

A guest had all kinds of activities available at Glen Eagles. There was a shooting school, which Jackie Stuart, the racing driver, had established. Mark Phillips and Princess Anne had started a riding club where I placed Steven and Emma Ford, who had spent four or five years in Abu Dhabi, falconing with Sheik Zayed.

In 1976, our first shoots took place on November 29th and 30th and from December 1st through 4th. We made a tremendous effort, and the results gave Keir a well-deserved reputation. In six days we bagged:

Pheasants	3,245
Grey partridges	147

Hare	125
Ducks	54
Rabbits	43
Geese	31
Woodcocks	30
Various	5
Total	3904 pieces

The ducks included gargany, goldeneye, mallard, merganser, pintail, rochard, shoveler, teal, tufted, and widgeon. The geese were either grey-legged or pink-footed.

The waterfowl were all wild, and the sight of thousands of geese landing on the Ardoch lochs in the evening was unforgettable.

Initially, when we were still staying at Castle Keir, one shooting party included:

Prince Michel and Princess Maria Pia of Bourbon-Parma
Dr. Annibale Scotti-Casanova
Jack and Drue Heinz ("57 Varieties")
Count Didi Kesselstatt
Count Roland de La Poype
Count Jean de Mailly-Nesle
Hubert and Terry Pantz
Marquis Carlos de Paul
Count François de Riocour
Harry and Gail Theodoracopoulos
Dominic Tutino

Counting Bill Stirling and me, we were ten nationalities. And this first shoot was a resounding success. We all enjoyed ourselves, our reputation was established, and bookings for the next year came pouring in. After a few years, we had 36 shooting days with 300 names to play with. In our best year, we shot over 20,000 pheasants. The Keir shoots became popular because the shooting was excellent, the food delicious, and the lodging supremely comfortable – all in beautiful country and with delightful people.

There was a five-day shoot in 1978 that I call the "Hungarian shoot", because so many of my Hungarian friends attended. The Guns were:

Mihály Dobozy	François de Riocour
Lajos Károlyi	Eric de Serigny
László Károlyi	Henri Chastel
Johnny Pálffy	Franzi Kienast
Mark Pejacsevich	Hubert Pantz
Paul Stephaich	Charles de Cossé-Brissac
Peter Stephaich	Georges Révay

Ginger and Leila Seafield

Nina, Countess of Seafield, was a close friend and a countess in her own right. Her husband was an elegant sportsman, Derek Studley-Herbert. Their eldest son Ginger, the present Earl of Seafield, was at that time Viscount Riedhaven. They would register at a hotel as Mr. Studley-Herbert, the Countess of Seafield, and Lord Riedhaven. The luggage porters never got it straight.

Totaling over 400,000 acres, the Seafield estate was one of the most extensive landholdings in Scotland. This vast domain in the valley of the River Spey had been inherited from the Findlater family, one of whom had drafted the document that provided for the union of England and Scotland in 1707.

The residence of the Earls of Seafield was Cullen House, a large castle filled with lovely English portraits of family members. Gainsboroughs and the like were everywhere to be seen.

The family also owned Kinvechy, a beautiful shooting lodge on the Spey with about fifteen bedrooms. That is where I shot my stag, caught my salmon, and missed my grouse, all on the same

Red grouse, Scotland's best-known game bird

day. In Scotland, to be a good sportsman you have to bag all three animals in one day.

Every year on the "Glorious Twelfth" of August, when grouse shooting began, Kinvechy Lodge would be teeming with family and friends. Stag hunting ("stalking")would begin around

September 15th, and there was also excellent trout and salmon fishing.

Kinvechy is where I shot two capercaillies, one with each barrel. It's surprisingly easy to miss these big birds, because they are usually flying faster than you think. We in Central Europe shoot the "caper" in the mating season, and with a rifle. We approach this extremely wary bird while he is singing his love song.

After the early death of Nina Seafield, I would shoot with Ginger and his lovely Anglo-Egyptian wife, Leila. Until recent

Capercaillie

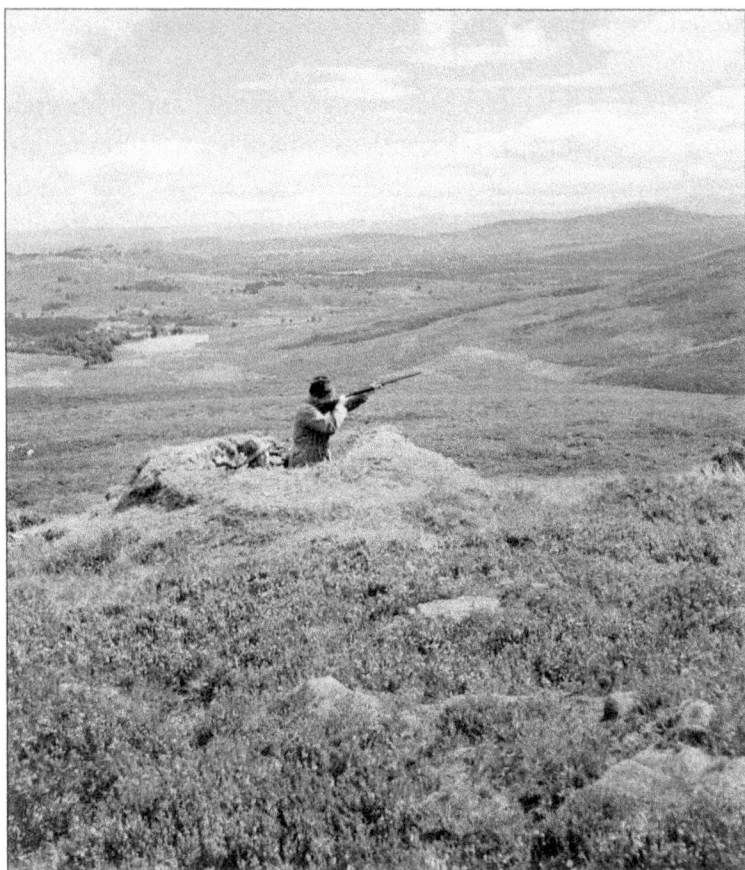
Shooting grouse from a butt near Kinvechy Lodge, Scotland

years, I visited with them regularly. Ginger is a wonderful host who can always be counted on to organize a good shoot, whether for pheasants, pigeons, or just clays. He has lovely black- and-white spaniel dogs, and his gamekeepers have their own tartan. I once asked a man what his job was, and he replied, "I'm a flanker at Lady Seafield's," by which he meant that his life's work was to serve as a beater on one flank of a drive.

At Kinvechy, the atmosphere is always perfectly congenial, and the many who work there worship the owners. The estate is expertly managed. Ginger is very knowledgeable and is also one of the nicest gentlemen I have met. Leila is very good-looking and a wonderful hostess. All the employees are perfectly attired. It is always a delight to be with Ginger and Leila. They love each other, and you can feel it when you enter the house. They made approximately twenty apartments in Cullen House, and they now live in what used to be the factor's lodge. They remodeled their new home in excellent taste, with their decorator friend Nina Campbell attending to the details. I feel very lucky to have been friends with this delightful family for over forty years.

The d'Arenberg Family

Menetou-Salon was an estate that belonged to Prince Charles d'Arenberg and his brother, Prince Armand. They divided the château, and each had his own friends and shoot. I was lucky to be friends with both brothers, and I shot with both of them for years.

The Château of Menetou-Salon, country seat of the Princes d'Arenberg

Charles married a beautiful American heiress, Peggy Bancroft, born Bedford, a Standard Oil heiress. She was an extraordinary beauty and a very special friend of mine. She had the best taste and was very kind, generous, and great fun. Their only child, Pierre, inherited not only Menetou, with its 3,000 acres, but also the fine qualities of both his parents. Pierre is one of the best and greatest hosts and a wonderfully loyal friend.

At the d'Arenbergs, there was always a duck drive, with the Guns placed behind a lane of high trees. But there was too much woodland and the terrain was rather flat, so it was difficult to produce high-flying birds.

It was always delightful to go to Menetou-Salon. The company was charming. The Countess of Paris, who shot very well with her 20-gauge guns, frequented this shoot, and what a *grande dame* she was.

At Menetou, there were beautiful stables and a hunt for red deer stags. The staghounds were always perfectly trained. Pierre d'Arenberg bought from his cousin the other half of the château and redecorated it with exceptional taste. He was married "at home" to his charming wife, born Countess Silvie de Castellane. Their marriage was an extraordinary event. Before arriving at the château, every car stopped at a buffet, where a glass of champagne and a caviar sandwich were given to the guest. Italian falconers on horseback entertained us with displays of falconry. We then sat down to lunch in an exquisite marquee, built for the occasion.

Hubert and Terry Pantz

Baron Hubert Pantz was the part-owner and manager of beautiful Mittersill Castle, in Austria. His partners were Prince Radic Lobkowicz and Count Hans Czernin. Golf, shooting, riding, and skiing were all available. Hubert's great friend Alex

Hohenlohe and his wife, "Honey Child," would receive and entertain the guests.

After Prince Bernhard and his bride, the future Queen Juliana of the Netherlands, spent their honeymoon at Mittersill, everyone who was internationally known passed through there – Paul Getty, Nubar Gulbenkian, Bing Crosby, Bob Hope, Clark Gable, Empress Soraya of Iran, the Aga Khan, and so on. Money and titles...

Terry Pantz had been married five times and would just call Hubert "the Fifth". She had become the widow of a Mr. McConnell, the founder of Avon Products. Since the Pantzes had no children, they spent their money to make their friends happy in the most generous way.

Hubert eventually disposed of Mittersill Castle to the Billy Graham Foundation and bought, with money from Terry's stepson Neil McConnell, the sixteenth century castle of Enzesfeld from Eugène de Rothschild. With wealth and taste, the Pantzes created a little paradise that offered stables for twenty horses, 1,200 acres of land with golf, shooting, a swimming pool and tennis courts, all just forty-five minutes from the Vienna Opera.

For years, I visited the Pantzes in May for the backgammon week that was organized by Mary Obolensky, partridge week in September, and pheasant week in November, which included two or three days of shooting in Czechoslovakia. Enzesfeld was large enough for thirty guests. We were in black tie for dinner, with Gypsy music and friends from Vienna and thereabouts.

The Pantzes had beautifully run homes in Marbella, Gstaad, Paris, and New York. Hubert and Terry eventually sold their house in rue de Bac, Paris, and moved, in the late 1970s, to 54 avenue d'Iéna, where I had lived before Louise and I were divorced. I had *carte blanche* to stay with the Pantzes anytime I wanted, meals included. Their butler, Baron Jean, and his wife, Thérèse, became good friends of mine. As I was again a bachelor, I found a new home. "You know where the kitchen is and where the bar is," they told me, "so don't ask stupid questions. Help yourself!"

Hubert shot with me in England and Spain. He was game for anything that was fun. My friends François de Riocour, Peter Salm, and Didi Kesselstatt received the same hospitable treatment from him.

Girls of various nationalities and colors were never in short supply at Hubert's parties. At his Arc de Triomphe luncheons for 150 people, half of the guests – those that went to the races – were served at 12:00 noon. At 2:30, there was a second seating for those who wanted to watch the races on television and then play gin rummy, bridge, or backgammon. No one could outdo Hubert and Terry at entertaining friends in such luxury and with such hospitality.

Edmond de Rothschild

After the Ganays, Edmond de Rothschild was the second person who invited me to shoot without having met me. He had heard that there was a Hungarian who had just arrived in France and liked to shoot, so he asked me to his lovely country seat at Armainvillier, an hour east of Paris.

Edmond was the only son of Baron Maurice de Rothschild, who was also an only son. Edmond's family bought him out of his partnership in the Rothschild Bank, and he left for the U.S.A. before World War II. He made another fortune there and became the wealthiest member of his family. Edmond had only one son, Benjamin, so his fortune remained in one hand. Edmond's second wife, the mother of Benjamin, is a very efficient, hard-working, and interesting lady who writes, appears on television, and is very popular in France.

Edmond became a friend of mine, and I shot with him for ten years. He always had interesting guests and amusing friends. I remember the drives in his game park, where the number 6 and 7 stands were the best. On a good day, I would shoot 60 or 70 birds in a drive. Evenings, we always had a fabulous dinner with the finest Château Lafitte wines, which are produced by the Rothschild family. A frequent shooting guest was President Georges Pompidou of France, a pleasant, easygoing gentleman who had previously been president of the Rothschild Bank. Edmond would sometimes place me next to Pompidou in the drive. If a good high pheasant was shot, Edmond would shout, "Bravo, Monsieur le Président!" And Pompidou would reply, "I know who shot that bird. It was the Hungarian."

On Edmond's shoot, I recall that some of the other Guns included Prince Bernhard of the Netherlands, Maurice Papon (the former prefect of Paris), Prince Charles d'Arenberg, François Péreire, Jean Sainteny, and Marc Henrion. We would shoot between 400 and 600 birds – pheasants, ducks, and some partridges. Edmond was a kind gentleman whose hospitality I could never forget.

Gyuri and Sonya Nemes

I met Gyuri Nemes and his wife, Sonya, both Hungarian, shortly after Louise and I arrived in France. Gyuri had worked for the French Rothschilds, in Morocco. Sonya's cousin Alix had been Guy de Rothschild's first wife.

There was always Hungarian hospitality at their country place, La Garenne, north of Beauvais. Gyuri made a 300-acre game park for moufflon (European wild sheep) and wild boars. Nothing was good enough for Gyuri, so he bought a huge wild boar, for breeding, from the Duke of Bavaria. There were three other boars in his park, and they were fighting all the time. Gyuri decided to shoot the younger boars and leave the big Bavarian tusker to do the breeding. He spotted a boar and after some hesitation, pulled the trigger. We walked up and found the great ducal boar lying dead. We went home with long faces, but managed to drown our disappointment with several glasses of Lafitte.

Gyuri then rented an estate, not far from Sandricourt, called Messlan, which had been Goelet property before World War II. Hans Czernin, Maurice Mohl, and Arnault de Monbrizon were the other shareholders. We would bring our children there along with some friends, a good picnic, and Katie, our Hungarian vizsla retriever.

We always tried to find an excuse to go to La Garenne. Archduke Ferdl Habsburg, Prince Alexander of Yugoslavia, and a group of Austrians were the regular guests, and Sonya cooked fabulous dinners. The days we spent with the Nemeses are treasured memories.

Peter and Wili Salm

After the Hungarian Revolution of 1956, I found my old friend Móric Nádosy and his family in an Austrian refugee camp. Another old friend of ours, Peter Salm, had inherited a lovely estate, named Port of Missing Men, in Southampton, New York. Peter's grandfather Henry Rogers was an associate of John D. Rockefeller, Sr., and one part of Peter's magnificent colonial house dated back to the seventeenth century.

When I asked Peter if he could use an accomplished gamekeeper with a family, he cabled back: "Send them to me." So Móric Nádosy immigrated with his wife and two children to America. Serious shooting then began at the Port of Missing

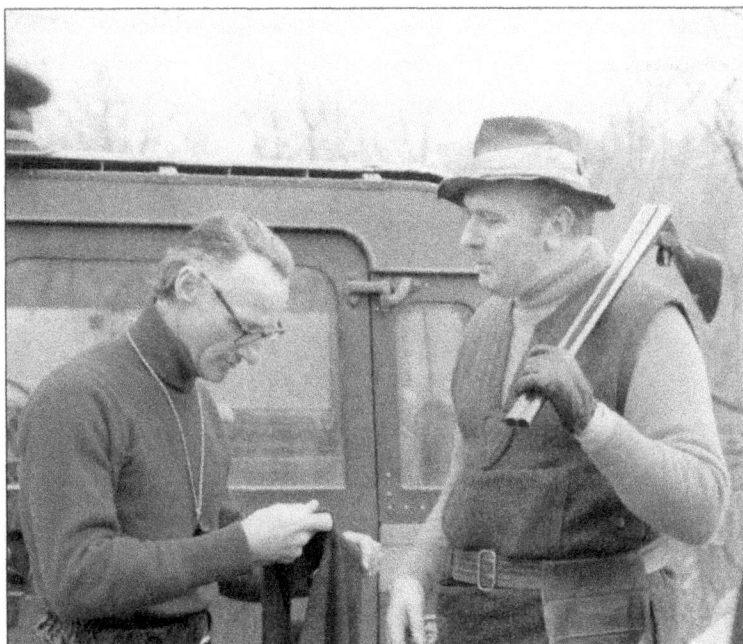

With Peter Salm at the Port-of-Missing-Men, Southampton, Long Island

Men. Mrs. Nádosy was in charge of the kennel and did some housework. The children were placed in very good schools.

I knew Peter's father, Ludi Salm, before and during the war. He was noted for two things. As a prisoner in World War I, he had been the tennis champion at Vladivostok, in Czarist Russia. His other memorable feat occurred in front of the old Sacher Hotel, in Vienna, where he struck Count Mihály Károlyi, the radical president of Hungary, two strong blows, right and left, shouting, "This one is for Austria! – the other for Hungary!"

But Ludi Salm came to a tragic end. In 1944, he was staying in the Hotel Ritz, in Budapest, when the concierge phoned upstairs to warn him that officers of the German Gestapo were in the elevator, going up to arrest him. He ended his life by jumping out of the window.

Peter's mother was the beautiful Millicent Rogers. As I mentioned earlier, the Duke of Spoleto, who was offered the crown of Croatia, had wanted to marry her, but Papa Rogers said, "No!"

Today, Peter's widow, Wili, and two attractive children, Antonia and Ludi, live at the Port. A few years ago, I and three

Peter Salm taking a high pheasant at the Port-of-Missing-Men

My friend Peter Salm

of our children rented and refurbished a small house on Cow Neck, a part of the Salm property, and spent a memorable summer there.

All of his friends miss Peter Salm, who died prematurely, in 1994. He was a true gentleman and a lifelong friend.

George Barcs

George Barcs was a Hungarian friend of mine and a knight of Malta. He had such a powerful aversion to paying taxes that for many years he posed as a resident of Monaco, where he had a profitable chemical factory. But he also had an apartment in Paris and owned part of a shoot, quite close to the city. The other owners included Jimmy Pourtales, the husband of a princess de Talleyrand whose mother was the American heiress Anna Gould.

I had a *carte blanche* invitation to shoot pheasants with George. The shoot was with released birds, but by October they were flying quite well. George wanted important personalities on his shoot, so I and my boss, Count Hans Czernin, rounded up a few archdukes and big industrialists. The ranking soldier of the French army, Maréchal Alphonse Juin, was invited quite often. His right hand had been crippled in the war, so he was quite dangerous to shoot with, especially for me, since George often placed me beside him "to make his bang sound louder." He accepted with pleasure the birds I shot for him.

Because of the fine wines that were always served, Le Maréchal would become quite talkative after lunch, and I had some interesting conversations with him. He had been partly responsible for the destruction of Monte Cassino, and the ferocity with which the enemy had fought to hold the venerable Benedictine abbey had left him profoundly impressed by the German army. I related to him my own military experiences; he was particularly interested in my contacts with the Free Poles at Warsaw, in 1944.

When George Barcs had to leave Monaco, he took refuge in the tax-free airport at Shannon, Ireland, and that was the end of my shooting with him.

I had originally met George through Christoph de Kállay, with whom, unfortunately, I never shot. Christoph's father had served as the last prime minister of Hungary, before the German occupation, and he had countersigned my appointment to the Foreign Office in 1944. Christoph went to Rome and served as ambassador of the Order of Malta to the Vatican. He became a friend of Pope John Paul II and was on many occasions of great service to people in need.

François de Riocour

In the 1960s, the shoot known as Zafra or Parador Hernán Cortés encompassed about 30,000 acres and belonged to the Ribeiro family of Guadalcanal, Spain. They would rent this shoot to Leo and Puppa Biaggi de Blasys, and Juan Ribeiro would manage it. Leo and Puppa also had a wonderful shoot of their own, known as Laronca.

Eventually, my dear and close friend Count François de Riocour rented Zafra from the Ribeiros, and I helped him develop this shoot into one of the finest in Spain. Summers were extremely hot, at Zafra, and the cattle, which were the only source of revenue, would nearly die, for there was almost no water and hardly any grazing. François and I persuaded the owners to stop raising cattle and to concentrate only on shooting. We got them to put in artesian wells, which supplied enough water for the birds, even in summer. We also hired gamekeepers to clean out the foxes, magpies, and birds of prey that lived on the partridges.

When we reached the point where we were shooting 20,000 partridges per season on 20,000 acres – 10,000 acres having been set aside for the birds to rest and breed in – we heard that the brothers Carlos and Pepe March had bought the entire estate.

At Zafra, the best drives were in the hilly parts of the property. The results for December 1971 and January 1972 were:

Shooting days:

December 6th, 7th, and 8th 1971	2,244 partridges
December 10th, 11th, and 12th 1971	2,668 partridges
January 3rd and 4th 1972	1,051 partridges
January 6th and 7th 1972	1,540 partridges
Total	7,503 partridges

Such were the results when we began to shoot at Zafra. After a few years, we were taking 20,000 birds a season. But we would stop shooting around January 15th, when the partridges began to mate. We were planning for the future.

Frequent shooting guests at Zafra included the following Guns:

Prince Pierre d'Arenberg

Prince Alfi Auersperg

Ambassador Sigismund Von Braun

Mrs. Jacques Firmen-Didot

Count Antal Forgach

Mr. John Goelet

Count de Guijas Albas

Mr. E. Heidsick

Mr. Marc Henrion

Prince Alfonso Hohenlohe

Count Didi Kesselstatt

Count Lichtenberg

Count Mariotti

Count Maurice Mohl

Prince Henri de la Tour d'Auverne
Count Johnny Pálffy
Baron Hubert Pantz
Count Dino Pecci Blunt
Count François de Riocour
Marquis Alain de Rosanbo
Viscount Paul de Rosière
Günther Sachs (the playboy)
Count Peter Salm
Dr. Annibale Scotti-Casanova
Mr. Paul Stephaich
Mr. Peter Stephaich
Colonel Bill Stirling
Mr. Beat Notz
The Duke of Urgel
Count Villanueva

We had terrific fun at Zafra, especially when we reached the point where we were shooting 800 birds a day. But it required a tremendous effort to get all of these Guns to participate, to take care of the payments, to look after arrangements with the *parador* (hotel), to keep our cars running and the cartridges flowing, to get a gunsmith in a hurry if one was needed, and to have a shady spot prepared for our luncheon, which would be catered by the Jockey Club or by Horcher, both first-class restaurants in Madrid. In addition to the Guns, there would always be between six and twelve non-shooters following along, mainly women who needed hairdressers and massages.

As you can see from the list of Guns, we shot with very few Spaniards. Their shooting habits were very different from ours. They would shoot any partridge, sometimes even ones that were running on the ground, just to surpass the other Guns in the number of birds killed. The "secretaries," who picked up the birds,

Red-legged partridge, Spain's best-known game bird

would make bets on whose boss would shoot the largest number. Often, they would race each other to pick up someone else's bird. As I noted previously, even Spanish duchesses would scoot out of their butts to snatch up birds killed by the other Guns.

Ordinarily, we would have five drives a day, and each drive would cover about 1,000 acres. François de Riocour's Coletta, who was always smoking a cigar, and my dear Don Gregorio were the senior loaders. I remember that Don Gregorio would sometimes sleep in front of my bedroom door so that no one would disturb me.

We never announced the total number of birds for any Gun. Our custom was to give birds to lady Guns and to those who wanted to look like the "top Gun".

We had a very sporty attractive extra girl, Princess Stephanie Windisch-Graetz. She would walk all day without shoes, as she had always done in Kenya. Stephanie spoke perfect Swahili and some other native languages. Her father, Franzi, was a great-grandson of Emperor Franz Joseph of Austria-Hungary. He lived near Nairobi and his house was filled with record-class trophies. One room was "wallpapered" entirely with lion skin. He had shot so many birds that the colonial government passed the *Lex Windisch-Graetz* limiting the daily bag of ducks and sand grouse.

Hubert Pantz once asked me to persuade Franzi Windisch-Graetz to shoot with us in Czechoslovakia. When I contacted him, he immediately asked me how many birds we could expect to shoot there. I said between 1,000 and 2,000 pheasants. His next question was, "Per Gun or per day?"

In the shoots at Zafra, if I did not satisfy everyone's needs, the operation would not work. For instance, there would be different groups for lunch and a strict order of precedence in the eating arrangements:

1. The Guns would eat in tents and only with their guests.

2. The loaders would eat separately, because they were not permitted to mingle with the Guns and refused to mingle with the beaters and picker-up boys.

3. There would be separate tables for the beaters because they would not mingle with the picker-ups.

4. Other tables were provided for the picker-ups, whom no one would mingle with.

With my loader, Don Gregorio, in Spain

The enjoyment of alcohol had to be strictly controlled. A loader who drank too much *chinchón* could be extremely dangerous when standing behind you and fumbling cartridges into two shotguns.

Luckily, in all those years at Zafra, we did not have a single accident. The only close call was when one of the Guns threatened to shoot the headwaiter, because the white wine was not cold. He never shot with us again.

Claude and Natalie Foussier

My friend Claude Foussier was an accomplished businessman – the distributor of Coca-Cola for France – but he stood out even more as a sportsman. He was the world champion shot and had headed the French national trap team, which included François de Riocour and Robert Melinette. He participated in the great international tournaments and brought glory and good will to France. He was also an excellent live pigeon shot and won many awards. His family had a shoot in the Sologne, where I shot with him for the first time in the 1960s.

Claude was often preoccupied with business and needed someone to manage his shooting. I arranged for Colonel Kit Egerton, a former British cavalryman whom I had known for several years, to take care of this job. Kit was running a shooting agency, called Sport Select, with James Holt, who was also a Yorkshireman. He had gained recognition by managing the shoot of Prince Stash Radziwill, at Helmsley, and Warter Priory for Stavros Niarchos, both famous shoots in Yorkshire.

In later life, Claude shot just as well with a 28-gauge over-and-under Perazzi gun as with a 12-gauge. He always had the same good loader and labrador retriever, and he shot with amazing accuracy and hardly ever winged a bird. His experience and knowledge about shooting made him one of the most outstanding shots of his day. Once in a while, he would even shoot with a 410-gauge gun.

Marc and Rosamée Henrion

Sasnières was a shoot that belonged to Mrs. Marc Henrion, born Rosamée de Brantes. Marc is a perfectionist, and in five or six years he turned Sasnières into the best artificial shoot that

Tableau of a shoot at Sasnières, the Henrion family château

Sasnières. chasse du samedi 9 décembre 1972

Tableau

488 coqs

305 poules

7g3

262 canards

63 perdreaux

1118

Fusils

Monsieur Alfredo Behrens Dalla Costa
Madame Albat Fabre
Comte Christian de Pils
Monsieur Pierre Hottinguer
Colonel Innes

Monsieur François Pereire
Comte François de Pourtalès
Vicomte Paul de Rosière
Comte Peter Salm
Monsieur Georges Cranchant

Guns who shot at Sasniéres, December 9, 1972, and the tableau

existed in France during the 1970s. He would drive pheasants, ducks, and partridges over two manmade lakes and would make them fly high and fast. I remember the first shoot, when we bagged only 23 birds. Six years later, we were shooting more than 1,300. Rosamée was a lovely hostess and a charming lady. I have only good memories of the Henrions.

Pepe Ramón Mora-Figueroa

One day, Bill Stirling told me that his friend Pepe Ramón Mora-Figueroa had asked to talk to him about something important. Pepe Ramón was married to a scion of the well-known Domecq family and was the chairman of its holding company. The family, which held the concession for Coca-Cola in Spain, would eventually buy out the Bronfman liquor business and was, of course, traditionally a producer of sherry.

Pepe Ramón and Count Bunting de Teba were two of the finest shots of their day. They shot partridges, ducks, and high pheasants equally well – which is rare, because normally a Gun specializes in one kind of shooting.

Pepe started a partridge shoot at Los Quintos, an estate in Andalusia, with five other friends, all excellent shots and very rich. The rules were strict. You were allowed to invite a guest only if you were present yourself. Consequently, once in a while, this territory was shot with only four Guns.

Los Quintos covered about 20,000 hectares. Efficient keepers were brought in to kill off the vermin and predators, and in two or three years the estate was producing 500 birds a day. In eight or ten years, the kill had risen to 1,000.

Bill Stirling kindly took me with him to Los Quintos, where we were invited for a one-day shoot. When we arrived, Pepe told us discreetly that for a good price he was prepared to sell the entire estate, along with a house for sixteen guests and a second house for twenty loaders, beaters, servants, and the like. Pepe thought that Bill, with his Arab contacts, might find the rich sheik that we're all looking for to buy Los Quintos. "By the way," said Pepe, "tomorrow we have a shoot starting at 11:00 A.M."

We were four Guns: Pepe and his son, Bill and I. At 11:00 A.M. sharp, the shoot began. We were firing 28-gram 65-millimeter cartridges and had excellent loaders. From the beginning, partridges were flying all over. It was quite a spectacle. Luckily, I shot well. After two hours, the only drive was over and we had bagged 900 birds among the four of us. Two hundred of them were mine. Pepe and his son shot brilliantly in what I remember as one of the landmark events of my shooting career.

Unfortunately, Bill did not find a buyer for Los Quintos. I had hoped that if he sold the estate, he might get permission to keep a shotgun there for himself and that he might let me use it once in a while.

In addition to being a very good Gun, Pepe Ramón was also an accomplished businessman. He gradually bought up the shares of the Domecq family company, and once he controlled it, he sold it to a British group that listed it on the London Stock Exchange under the name Allied Domecq. Later, I heard that its net worth had risen to two billion pounds – enough to buy a lot of partridges. Not long afterwards, Allied Domecq was bought by my friend Patrick Ricard for twelve billion pounds and is now quoted on the Paris Bourse under the name of Pernod Ricard.

Shoots I Remember Fondly

Kinnaird Castle

At Brechin, in Aberdeenshire, is Kinnaird Castle, the home of one of Britain's most sporting and elegant gentlemen, Charles Carnegie, 11th Earl of Southesk. I never met Charles's father, the 10th Earl, but he is remembered as one of the most accomplished

Still the happy hunter

Guns of all time. He once bagged 48 grouse with 48 shots. On that occasion, he missed one bird but bagged two others with one shot. He also shot 63 partridges with 63 shots, bagged 79 pheasants without a miss, and killed 228 pheasants with 238 cartridges in 17 minutes, which amounted to a dead bird every 5 seconds. He was one of a party that shot 51 capercaillies at Kinnaird.

The days of such bags are mostly gone, but Kinnaird was still an outstanding shoot when my group hunted there. I no longer recall whether Lajos Károlyi or Peter Salm initially contacted the earl, but I organized our shoot. We stayed in a nearby hotel, rather than in the castle, because we had some extra girls and didn't want to embarrass the host.

I must tell you about our luncheons in the cellar of the castle. The earl would be seated at the head of the long dining table, with his butler, in cutaway, standing behind him. The rustics who picked up the dead birds would be awkwardly seated in two lines on the earl's right and left. He and his group would be served with royal flatware, for his first wife had been Princess Maud, a granddaughter of King Edward VII. At the other end of the long table sat the wretched "continentals" – Prince Auersperg, Prince Hohenlohe, Count Salm, Count Károlyi, and Baron Pantz, all eating with metal flatware on cheap throwaway china. Still worse, the earl had placed two empty chairs on either side of the table to insulate his group from ours!

This was demeaning enough, but on top of everything there were too few birds. So we asked the earl to give us a free duck shoot the following morning. We got up at 6:00 A.M., went out, and did not shoot a single duck. The gamekeeper later admitted that the earl had ordered him to release no ducks. We decided to take our revenge. During luncheon, Prince Auersperg said to Prince Hohenlohe in a deliberately loud voice, "Alex, you should not have killed that swan this morning! You know that the swans are Her Majesty's birds!" And Prince Hohenlohe replied in an equally loud voice, "All right, Alfi, I killed that swan, but you wounded two in a row!" The earl practically turned blue in the face. We finally told him that the story was just a "continental" joke and that we should remain friends, which we did.

Invermark

This famous shoot and the nearby grouse moors of Round Hill, Millden, and Ganakie were owned by Simon Ramsay, 16th Earl of Dalhousie, the brother-in-law of my friend Bill Stirling. All four were in Aberdeenshire, near Brechin, where the earl had his residence. The largest was Invermark, which covered about 70,000 acres and was quite near Balmoral.

After World War II, Lord Dalhousie rented his shoots to the Marquis Henri de Boigelin, a distinguished French sportsman. Henri would move to the moors on the "Glorious Twelfth" of August, when grouse shooting begins, and remain there till December 12th, when it ends. In due time, the organization of so much shooting became bothersome, so Henri decided to give the Ganay family a week of shooting at Invermark, and they eventually decided to let our mutual friend Peter Salm shoot there too. If necessary, the Ganays would exchange Guns with Salm, and that is how I came to be invited by them and also by Salm to shoot at Invermark from about 1960 to 1985. In those years, on a good day, the bag of grouse would exceed 200 brace, or 400 birds, with eight Guns.

I remember an amusing mishap that took place at Invermark. The Duke of Roxburghe – known as "Bobo" – had served with Bill Stirling in the Strategic Air Services (SAS) during World War II. They decided that if they survived the war, they would rent the best grouse moor for one week every year. They rented Invermark. But, in the lovely shooting lodge, the duke found that he had a room without an attached bathroom. He complained, but there was a slight misunderstanding; the following year when he arrived, there was a bathtub in his bedroom. Furthermore, because the duke was very heavy, the butler and an assistant had to push and pull him to get him out of the tub. They never thought of a shower.

Invermark was a dream. With its lovely lodge, so many wonderful friends, superb shooting, and incomparable food and service, Invermark was as near to heaven as one could get on earth.

Apart from Peter Salm and the Ganays, some of the habitual Guns at Invermark were my close friends Count Didi Kesselstatt, Commander Toby Marten, Viscount Ginger Riedhaven, John Goelet, Colin Campbell, Count Feri Széchenyi, and Prince Moritz Oettingen.

Rothwell

A perfectionist and highly successful businessman, Sir Joe Nickerson built up an excellent pheasant and partridge shoot at Rothwell, in Lincolnshire. He liked to shoot at home with four or five friends, among them the crack shot Claude Foussier. The first drive would start at 11 A.M., and by 4 P.M. we would be having tea before the roaring fireplace while 400 to 500 birds lay in rows on the front lawn. I think Sir Joe's shoot set the British record for grey partridges when five Guns bagged over 2,000 birds in one day. The regular Guns at Rothwell would include Prince Charles and Princess Anne of Great Britain and Prince Bernhard of the Netherlands.

In his fourth wife, Eugenie, who was Guatemalan, Sir Joe finally found a lady who liked to shoot and who could put up with his personality. When they came to my friend Bill Stirling's shoot, the Nickersons would arrive in grand style and comfort.

Sir Joe Nickerson on his Rothwell estate

First would come a Land Rover with Sir Joe's butler, his loaders, his suitcases, guns, and shooting gear, so that when he and Eugenie arrived, their clothes would already be unpacked and ironed. Their Rolls-Royce was equipped with a telephone, and Sir Joe even carried a dictaphone to record his financial brainstorms.

Finally, a second Land Rover would pull up with a gamekeeper in charge of the master's labradors.

Sir Joe also had a couple of grouse moors. One was near Lord Peel's property in Yorkshire, and he left it to his wife with a trust fund to cover its maintenance. I remember shooting there with Sir Joe and later with Eugenie. It was a very fine moor, but not comparable to the best ones in Scotland.

Shooting with Jani Róth at Glenlivet and on the River Avon

I met Jani Róth when I was still in Hungary. He had owned a shooting agency but had left Hungary, at the right moment, with some money, and had settled in London. They say that money makes money, and Jani was a good example of that. He had a fancy office in Berkeley Square, which became the meeting place of the expatriate Hungarian aristocracy – free food, free drinks...

Jani rented a shoot from Richard Waddington, who lived in Scotland, at Glenlivet, which is famous for its whisky. He invited me, my brother, Paul, and my brother-in-law, Billy Hitchcock, to shoot with him. Including the other guests, we came to eight Guns and were an interesting group. Some of the invited guests were first-timers on the moors. Poor Aurora Hitchcock, who didn't know better, arrived wearing a very smart snow-white fur coat, to the utter horror of the veteran Guns. We gave her an old-fashioned loden coat, and all was forgiven.

It was late in the season, so the grouse were "packed". Big coveys would fly over, so the bag was not large. But everyone had a good time. In the evenings, we would play bridge, and the world's finest whisky helped to maintain the atmosphere.

Jani Róth wanted to convince the Scots that one can have good pheasant shooting in Scotland. But by mid-November there is often snow at the higher elevations, which makes the pheasants reluctant to rise. Thousands of pheasants had been released, and poor Jani had to admit that pheasant shooting in the Highlands is "for the birds." That said, with a fun group we still enjoyed ourselves.

I remember the time that Jani invited the late Earl of Lucan to shoot with us. Lucan's great-grandfather was the officer who had delivered the erroneous order to Lord Cardigan, at Balaclava, that triggered the Charge of the Light Brigade. That Lucky Luke, as we called the earl, was just as capable of indiscretion as his famous ancestor is confirmed by the following anecdote.

Jani claimed to have shot a woodcock on the far side of the River Avon, and when the current proved to be too strong for our labradors to swim across, Lucky Luke made a nasty remark about Hungarian truthfulness. As a friend of Jani's and upset by Lucan's arrogance, I took my shepherd's stick and waded across the river, which was up to my shoulders. On the far side, thank God, I found the woodcock. Clutching it between my teeth like a bird dog, I retrieved it, while the other Guns, loaders, and beaters cheered and shouted encouragement. I was blue in the face with cold, but Hungarian honor had been saved! I went to our lodgings, had a hot bath, and drank tea with plenty of Scotch. I didn't even catch cold. Wonderful to be young!

A few years later, Lord Lucan shot and killed his children's governess in their London townhouse. Rumor has it that he mistook the governess for his wife, who was trying to divorce him. He then disappeared and was never seen or heard of again. Lucky Luke's luck had run out.

Allonsville

Allonsville was a gray partridge shoot and one of the best in France. It belonged to Prince Jean de Caraman-Chimay and his wife, born Jacqueline Hennessy, but it was rented to the Ganay family. The captain of this shoot was the Duke of Mouchy, a brother of Philippine de Ganay. The Ganays had four or five Guns; the rest they gave out to friends like the Rothschilds and to Sir Christopher Soames, the British ambassador.

Once, Prince Charles, the heir to the British throne, came to shoot as a guest of the Soameses. Our hotel did not want to give him a room, for he was traveling incognito and did not have his passport. The detectives, who had been hiding in the cornfields during the shoot, came to his rescue and solved the problem. We had a good laugh.

I also remember that Lord Tony Lambton came once in a business suit, but he was still permitted to shoot – and shot extremely well, as always.

On another occasion, Ambassador Soames bought up all the partridges for a dinner he was giving for the three cousins, Princess Alexandra of Kent, Archduchess Helen of Austria, and Prince Alexander of Yugoslavia, in the historic and beautiful British Embassy, which had belonged to Napoleon's sister, Princess Pauline Borghese.

A Boar Shoot with Duke Albrecht of Bavaria

I have the most delightful memories of my shoot for wild boars with H.R.H. Duke Albrecht of Bavaria. Had his grandfather Ludwig III not abdicated the throne in 1918, Albrecht would have been king of Bavaria.

Duke Albrecht's history was extraordinary. He left Germany when Hitler came to power in 1933 and took refuge in Brazil with his Hungarian wife, born Countess Mária Draskovich, and their four children. Later, he was placed in charge of all the shoots in Yugoslavia by the regent of that country, Prince Paul. All went well, until Hitler occupied Yugoslavia in 1941. Compelled to flee once again, the duke took refuge in his wife's country. Count Kálmán Tisza owned 3,000 hectares and a shooting lodge just outside Budapest, and he invited Duke Albrecht and his family to stay there. But again, Hitler was not far behind. In March 1944, the Germans occupied Hungary, and the duke found himself with no avenue of escape. He and his family were packed off to the Dachau concentration camp, where they spent the rest of the war trying to survive. When the camp was liberated by Allied troops, my friend Pierre Vernes was the one who opened the door of Duke Albrecht's cell.

For that memorable boar shoot, I flew to Munich with my old friend Prince Abdorreza Pahlavi of Iran, and from there on

European wild boar

we had a royal experience. Among the guests were many Guns from Central Europe, including a number of Hungarians, as well as many German dukes and princes. I thoroughly enjoyed myself but was unlucky and shot only one boar.

Berleburg

Some years ago, my friend Robin Wittgenstein invited me to hunt boars on the 15,000-acre shoot of his brother, Prince Richard zu Sayn-Wittgenstein, at Berleburg, in Germany. We would have one drive in the morning, followed by a picnic luncheon in the open, with big fires to warm us. There were no drives in the afternoon. The territory was so large that I never saw anything to shoot. But every evening there was a spectacular dinner, with the guests all seated at one long table. King Gustav of Sweden and the host's sister-in-law, Queen Margrethe of Denmark, were also present. The ladies wore long dresses with diadems or tiaras. A galaxy of illustrious names from the Almanac of Gotha attended.

Friedrichsruh

My friend Ferdinand Bismarck is a great-grandson of the celebrated Iron Chancellor, Prince Otto von Bismarck, who conquered the Austro-Hungary Empire at the Battle of Königgrätz, in 1866, and the French Empire of Napoleon III at Sedan, in 1870. More important, he forged a disparate collection of kingdoms, dukedoms, and principalities into a unified German Empire and placed the King of Prussia on the imperial throne. The German Empire has disappeared, but the unified Germany is an enduring monument to the Bismarck family.

The shoot was perfectly organized. We were a multinational group of at least 30 Guns. They drove us from stand to stand in

Friedrichsruh, country seat of the Bismarck family

ten Volkswagen buses with Porsche engines. I bagged four or five boars, but none with trophy tusks. To be frank, I shot badly, but then, I've never been nearly as accurate with a rifle as with a shotgun.

In the evenings, we were treated to a sumptuous dinner. There was music, and the presence of so many gorgeous long-legged Teutonic girls made a riveting impression.

Shidlokovice

In the spring of 1970, I received an invitation from Jack Heinz, the catsup czar, to shoot pheasants at Shidlokovice, in Czechoslovakia. He was thoughtful and sent the invitation months in advance. I had heard a great deal about Shidlokovice and was excited about the prospects.

It was a government-owned shoot with a large castle that had belonged to Archduke Friederich of Austria-Hungary before World War I. The castle had been divided in half so that two groups could be shooting at same time. Each half had about fifteen bedrooms and baths, a large living room with a fireplace, a dining room for twenty-five people, and a small drawing room for parlor games, reading, and watching television.

At dinner, we were not in black tie because the revolution of 1968 had just been repressed and Czechoslovakia had been forced back into strict communism. To shoot a few thousand pheasants a day was not exactly communistic, but it brought much-need dollars to the People's Democratic Republic.

I flew to Vienna with two shotguns and all my shooting gear but without cartridges; they could not be imported and had to be bought locally. Cars for us and trucks for the baggage were waiting at the airport. We had no customs problems in Vienna, but at the Czech border we had to wait for a couple of hours while the inspectors searched everything. Jack Heinz had some people who produced the different licenses, and eventually we arrived at Shidlokovice. Lots of trophies hung on the castle walls. There was a fire in every fireplace, and the service was good.

At dinner, we were given the program for the next morning: breakfast at 8:30, departure at 9:15. The terrain turned out to be quite flat and not very attractive. Our loaders were, I think, military people. We were also assigned people to carry our coats and cartridges. We were to shoot both cock and hen pheasants, and there was a man to count the number of birds shot. Predictably, his figures and ours were never quite the same, but our host had to pay for every bird that was officially counted. Often, when someone clearly missed a bird, the official counter would shout "Bravo!" and add one more bird to the count. There were many pheasants, and the official counter would noisily encourage me to shoot running birds. I replied that I would never shoot a running bird and that he should shut up because he was disturbing me.

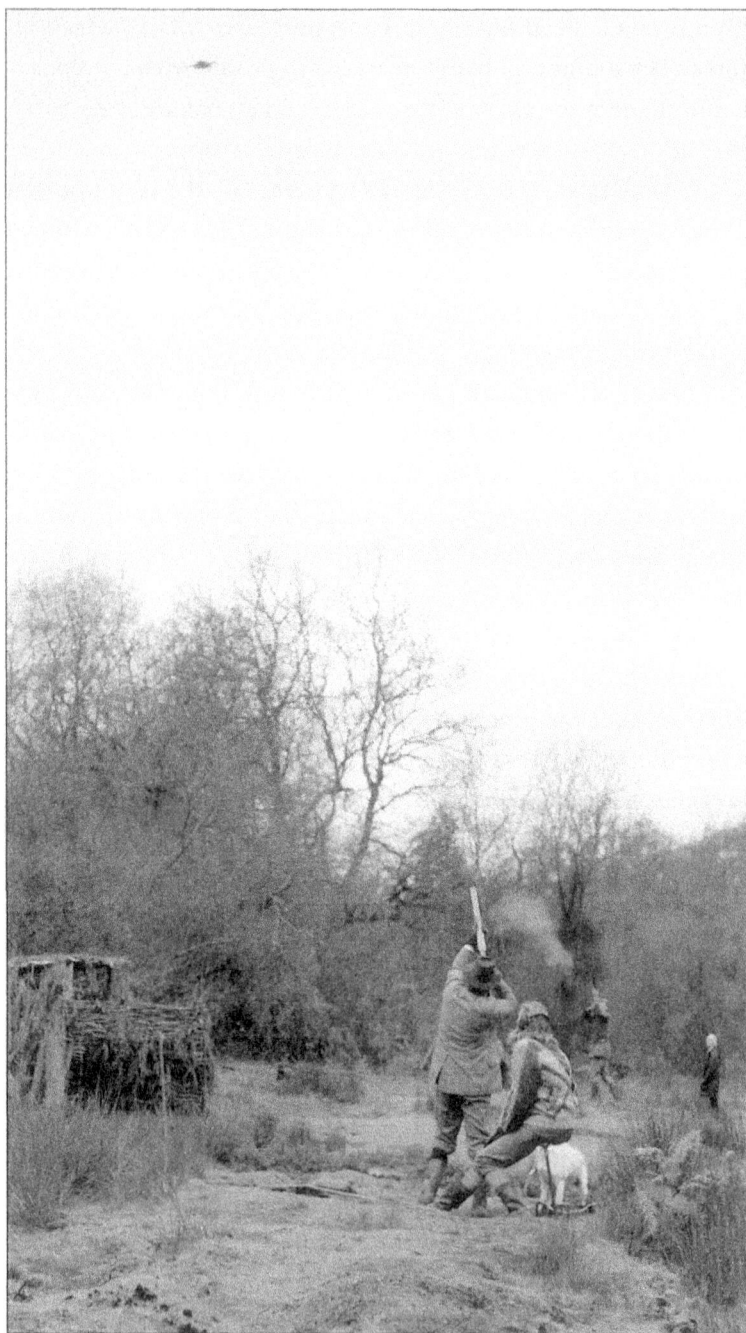

Taking a high pheasant

We had a simple luncheon in the field, with a fire, and after several glasses of quite good wine, the atmosphere became more pleasant.

We were ten Guns, mostly English and American. They included Hoyt Ammidon, the president of U.S. Trust of New York, the Hon. Angus Ogilvy and his beautiful wife, Princess Alexandra of Kent, the Hon. Hugh Fraser, MP for Scotland and a brother of my friend Lord Lovat, Fred Hamilton, an oil man from Denver, and others.

In the evening, there would be a big fire, and the Guns would line up while buglers played the old ceremonial tunes over the dead birds. I think it is a fine tradition that in Central Europe each kind of game animal has its own special melody, written by famous composers of the seventeenth and eighteenth centuries. All the gamekeepers and beaters were standing at attention, which provided a farewell salute to the 3,000 pheasants that were shot that day. The quality of the birds was not good, the quantity perhaps too great. I heard that a few weeks later another group shot 5,000 pheasants in one day, which confirms that the birds were of poor quality – too easy to shoot – and could not have provided good sport.

The next day, the territory we shot over was again completely flat. Without wanting to offend my host, I refused to shoot the low, easy birds. The official counter was furious.

Spetsopoula

This island of about 3,000 hectares was owned, in my time, by Stavros Niarchos, and his children own it now.

Louise and I were thrilled to receive an invitation to visit Spetsopoula, and we made our preparations: evening dress for dinner, bathing suit for the sea or pool. We flew to Athens, where a small dark gentleman asked for my passport. I hesitated

Moufflon (European wild sheep)

Fallow deer

to give it to him, because I had had so much trouble getting it. He told me that he was Mr. Niarchos' agent – that was a good enough reference. We were escorted into the VIP lounge, where refreshments and sandwiches were served. The same man then came to tell us that our luggage was cleared and asked whether we would like to go Spetsopoula by helicopter or on the famous sailing yacht Creole. We chose the 'copter, as the boat ride would have taken four or five hours.

On our arrival, we found the charming Eugénie Niarchos, born Livanos, waiting to show us our quarters. Every guest couple got a "cabana", comprising two bedrooms, a living room, a kitchen, and a maid who unpacked our luggage and ironed and cleaned for us. A small open Fiat stood in front of our cabana to take us to the Niarchos home for dinner. Eventually we found ourselves in the big dining room with the fireplace, where a number of paintings from Mr. Niarchos' famous collection hung on the walls and there were tables for bridge and backgammon after dinner. The other guests included Jack Heinz, the catsup maker, his wife, Drue, the Marquis de Villaverde, a son-in-law of the Spanish dictator General Franco, Leo and Puppa Biaggi de Blasys, and the Marquis di Guglielmi, who had a wild boar shoot outside Rome.

All of these people were hunters. Once you have a good shoot of your own, you invite the owners of other good shoots. Then they invite you to shoot with them. That's how a shooting group is built up.

On Spetsopoula we shot for two days – the first day pheasants and red partridges, the next day mouflon and fallow deer, with rifles.

Managed by a Danish keeper named Dino, the bird shooting was very good. The island is hilly and rocky, so once in a while we had to shoot downward, and some of the fast-flying partridges plummeted into the sea. Small boats were circling to pick them up. At certain stands, the pheasants would fly very high, and if you were placed in a valley, they would be almost out of range. We nonetheless shot around 500 partridges and 800 pheasants.

A fine luncheon was served at the swimming pool – lobster and other seafood. You could swim in the pool, have a massage, read the latest newspaper, and enjoy the drinks – a perfect organization and most pleasant atmosphere. The luncheon would last two hours. There was no rush!

After dinner, we played bridge or backgammon while the ladies chitchatted or listened to music. There was also a movie theater where the latest films were shown.

The next day came the big game hunt. Hundreds of mouflon were running back and forth, and some of the guests were shooting with two rifles. Altogether, we shot about 60 mouflon and 40 fallow deer.

For the return trip to Athens we took the *Creole*, one of the most beautiful yachts and fitted out with the most modern technical equipment. Mr. Niarchos came with us. When I asked him where his office was, he replied, "In my head."

This was probably the most luxurious shoot I ever attended. Everything was perfect, to the last detail. I was delighted that Louise came along. We had a truly extraordinary experience.

Ducks in the Nile Delta

As I mentioned earlier, Louise and I lived in Egypt for a brief period in 1956, and we loved it there.

Luckily, I was able to gain admission to the storied Club de la Chasse et du Pêche, which held the shooting rights for 100,000 acres of the Nile Delta. Due to the shortness of our stay and the increasing political troubles, I shot only once in Egypt. But that may have been my most interesting shoot.

We set out from Alexandria at 4:00 A.M. and drove to the Delta, where small boats, each rowed by two oarsmen, had been readied to convey us into the swamps. In addition to my gun, I was carrying 600 cartridges, a picnic lunch, and a thermos of tea. It took the boatmen half an hour to row me to my butt, which turned out to be a metal barrel sitting in the water and anchored in the mud. This barrel contained a wooden stool and some shelves on which to rest the cartridge boxes. The boatmen then rowed away, saying that they would return around 1:00 P.M.

As the hunting area was large, thirty or forty Guns had been placed at some distance from one another to keep the ducks from settling. The next Gun may have been one kilometer away. On calm days, a few of the Guns would be rowed out onto the Mediterranean to keep the birds from landing there.

At first light, the ducks would begin to fly and search for food. After an hour, there were thousands of waterfowl in the air – a sight very difficult to describe. There were pelicans, swans, several kinds of herons, and eight or ten kinds of ducks and geese, all circling overhead and making an almost deafening racket.

I had only one gun – a 12-gauge automatic – and I kept firing till my arm got tired. Eventually I took a rest and simply enjoyed the view. The next Gun was too far away for me to spot him, even through my binoculars, but once in a while, when the wind was right, I could hear him shooting.

The water was only 20 to 50 centimeters deep, but I had been warned not to leave my barrel because it was dangerous to walk in the mud and I was completely alone.

The incredible spectacle of the morning began to wind down around 11:00 A.M., when many ducks flew away to look for food in the inland grain fields. But even during this pause, there were still hundreds of birds in the air. And after about an hour, the ducks that had flown away started to come back from the fields, and the incomparable spectacle began again.

Though I shot badly at first, my final tally came to 250 birds, taken with only one gun. I refused to shoot swans, storks, herons, pelicans, and ibises. My neighbor Gun and friend Manolo Vafiades shot more than 450 birds that morning. A world champion live pigeon shot, he lived in Alexandria and had shot in the Delta many times.

Eventually, the boatmen rowed back to the butts, bringing young boys to pick up the dead birds and kill the wounded ones. I'm sorry that many birds could not be retrieved. We gave the ones that were picked up to a local hospital.

The Nile Delta is now a sanctuary, like the delta of the Danube, in Romania, and that of the Guadalquivir, in Spain. These are the three great sanctuaries for waterfowl in Europe.

Red Deer in the Andes

I have heard that before World War I, a German introduced two red deer stags and ten hinds into Argentina. Another German eventually bought these deer and began to breed them. Due to the very fine feed, favorable climate, and effective protection, the number of red deer increased, after twenty years, to a few hundred. Eventually, André de Ganay and a Belgian, Mr. Bracht, bought the estate where the deer had become established and continued to breed them. Today, many thousands of European red deer live on a few hundred thousand acres in the mountainous San Martín de los Andes region.

At the suggestion of my brother, Paul, who had already hunted deer in Argentina, I went to try my luck at shooting a gold medal stag – a new adventure. Our shoot was arranged by a Hungarian friend named Pista Lyka.

From New York to Buenos Aires to Bariloche and then by car to San Martín was a long journey in 1964. But at San Martín, Paul, and two friends, Antal Forgach and Franzi Kienast, were waiting for me.

My brother, Paul, with two magnificent red deer stags, taken in Argentina

After buying a two-week supply of wine, coffee, salami, paprika, and other essentials, the four of us set out for our first camp on horseback with two guides, a cook, and ten packhorses. As the tents were being pitched, Paul and I decided to take a walk. We eventually spotted two figures in the distance and proceeded to follow them. One turned out to be our good friend Michel de Ganay, who owned the next hunting area, or *coto*.

Another nearby *coto* was rented to an Austrian named Fritz Mandel. He had been president of an association of Austrian industrialists before World War II, but was better remembered as the husband of Hedy Lamarr, the actress. I met Hedy a few times. She was very beautiful, but once she opened her mouth her charm was gone. She had a terrible voice, was incredibly stupid, and finally died of alcoholism.

Mandel had some Hungarian guests, the Károlyis and Tuli Bethlen, so we visited each other's camps and exchanged our daily shooting experiences. We spent a delightful week in that particular *coto*, but we shot nothing of interest. I remember the giant condors gliding with open wings, like small airplanes.

From our camp in a valley near a river, we would ride up into the mountains every day around 5:00 A.M. Our horses were wonderful at climbing without roads or trails. I would give my horse the reins and watch him climb over tree trunks and rocky places – just up and up. Thank God we had no problems. We heard about a German named Schultz whose horse fell on his leg, and by the time he arrived at a hospital his leg had to be amputated. We were remote from any help – no medicine, no doctors, nothing.

At the camp of a friend of ours, Bandi Milos, a tragic incident occurred that ended with the death of his cook. Bandi was camped with his daughter, Andrea, her husband, Pierre Frottier, and our friend Lajos Károlyi. Their cook got drunk and went crazy. In the morning, he approached Andrea's tent clutching a long hunting knife and a machete. With his .22 rifle, Bandi fired a warning shot into the ground near the cook's feet, but he would not stop. Bandi then shot the cook in the chest and killed him.

A crowd of the dead man's friends and relatives came up from the village and were ready to attack the Europeans. Fortunately,

Red deer stag in Argentina

Lajos Károlyi was able to summon some soldiers while the Europeans, with rifles in hand, kept the villagers at bay. The soldiers told the villagers that Bandi was under arrest, which quieted them, and they returned to their village. Everybody agreed that Bandi had acted in self-defense, and after paying a fine, he was set free. The hunt was of course canceled.

We eventually changed camp and went to the *coto* of Colungo, where there was a lovely river and beautiful woods but very few stags roaring. The weather was lousy – snow and freezing temperatures. One night, our tent blew away and left Paul and me in our sleeping bags in a driving rainstorm. Suddenly strangers arrived and said they were lost. One was Adolf Spuhlberg, a well-known Belgian. I gave him my sleeping bag and crawled in with my brother. Every time I see Adolf, he reminds me of that episode.

I shot a few mediocre stags, nothing interesting. Every day was dangerous because of rain and the slippery slopes. We visited André de Ganay, who gave a big *asado* – a kind of buffet-barbecue – for Princess Lilian de Réthy. I had met her in 1939 when she was Lilian Baels, and I will have more to say about her later in my recollections of hunting at Hinterriss, her shoot in Austria. Occasionally we would invite Eny and Giorgio Matarazzo, who lived not far from our *coto*, to come to our camp. They were a very sporty couple who rode and fished and played polo with the local cavalry officers, all in lovely surroundings.

Though the weather was often filthy, we went out every day hoping to shoot a gold medal stag, unfortunately without success. Still, it was a memorable time because of the wonderful company. Each of us lost a few kilos, as the hunting was difficult and the food, miserable. We would visit our neighbors for dinner, they would come to our camp, and so time passed very pleasantly. I never got what I was hunting for – a gold medal stag. What I did get was the adventure of a lifetime.

We returned to Buenos Aires, visited our friends, and gave a dinner. Then, with beautiful memories, we left Argentina. I believe it is a country of the future and will be for the next hundred years.

Doves in Argentina

After my red deer hunt in Patagonia, I went to shoot doves with the Ganays at a spot not far from Córdoba.

It is interesting that in 1939 the German battleship *Graf Spee* was driven by British warships into the Plata River and scuttled by its captain. There were nearly 2,000 crew members, and the Argentine government did not know what to do with them. Many eventually settled around Córdoba, and today there are some 10,000 German-speaking Argentineans, the descendants of that crew. Hence, the hotel where we stayed at Córdoba was called the Hamburg.

An agency arranged a three-day dove shoot for Michel and Paul de Ganay and myself. In the morning, we would shoot the doves as they flew out from their roosting areas to feed in the fields. At midday, there would be relative calm. Then, around 3:00 P.M., the birds would start flying back from the fields to their roosting places. Thousands of them would fly out in the morning and back again in the afternoon.

None of us reached the magic number of 1,000 doves per Gun in one day, but I know a number of people who did. One member of the Spanish Domecq family shot by himself, with four 20-gauge automatic shotguns and an appropriate number of loaders and picker-ups, over 2,000 birds in a single day. It helped that his gas-operated automatic guns had no recoil, because he had to fire 3,000 cartridges. He had to shoot and pick up a bird every 20 seconds, which is quite a trick. He wanted to put himself into the Guinness Book of Records, but the waiting list was too long.

At Córdoba, in the hot season, you shoot so many shells that you have to cool your barrel with water, and you have to wear a thick winter glove to keep from burning your forward hand. Mornings and afternoons, there were hundreds of birds overhead, all flying very high and some flying crosswise. It was a memorable experience.

For quantity shooting, doves at Córdoba, ducks in the Nile Delta, and pheasants in Czechoslovakia will always come to mind.

Red Deer at Hinterriss with Princess Lilian de Réthy

Before the war, I had a Hungarian friend named Peter Draskovich. He was very fond of an extraordinary beauty named Lilian Baels, whose father was a local governor in Belgium. Lilian came to Hungary to visit Peter, but he had to explain that he could never marry her because it was written in the family testament that he had to marry a lady of noble birth or forfeit his inheritance – 10,000 hectares of farmland and woods on the Yugoslav border.

Lilian was deeply aggrieved and also quite angry. She returned to Belgium and not long afterward married King Leopold III; his late wife, the very popular Queen Astrid, was the mother of King Baudouin and King Albert. Lilian was created Princess de Réthy but was denied the title of queen.

I have already mentioned how my brother, Paul, and I met Lilian while hunting stags in Argentina. When I met her again, she remembered me and asked me to join her for a stag hunt at Hinterriss, her shoot in Austria, near Innsbruck. I accepted with pleasure, and there I met Ivan Maura, a well-known sportsman who organized hunts in Spain. I also met Count Páli Palffy, a great and very good-looking gentleman who helped Princess Lilian organize Hinterriss, with its 20,000 acres, for hunting red deer, chamois, and roe. His son, Johnny Palffy, had attended our wedding in 1954.

Hinterriss was a very attractive shoot, but in the Austrian mountains the stags' antlers are not very strong thanks to poor nourishment. I nonetheless shot two stags and two chamois, which was what the gamekeeper permitted me.

Over the hill was another part of Hinterriss, which was rented by Alain and Élie de Rothschild. Louise and I were invited there by Élie, and we stayed for a few lovely days. This shoot was perfectly managed by five bearded gamekeepers, and we enjoyed it a great deal. I shot one stag there.

Sir Jimmy MacAlpine's Shoot in Wales

Sir Jimmy was a wealthy South African industrialist who owned a Welsh estate where we shot a few times.

Once, during luncheon, I found myself seated beside Lady MacAlpine, in a restaurant. Whenever she was served, she would start to giggle. I asked her what the giggling was about, and she replied that it amused her to be served because she had recently been a waitress in that very restaurant and the other waitresses had been her peers. "Good for you!" I said. Otherwise, our shoot was uneventful.

Bobwhite Quail in Georgia

Before our marriage in 1954, Louise had a great friend named Fred Hamilton, who invited us to shoot quail with him on his estate in Georgia, Seminole Plantation. This property had previously belonged to Ambrose Clark, an heir to the Singer (Sewing Machine) Company. Louise had to decline at the last moment, so I went with my French friends Marc and Rosamée Henrion. A stockbroker named Bill Hutton, his wife, and our host and hostess made up the group. I had never shot quail in the U.S.A., so I was very curious.

The Hamiltons' house was comfortable, even luxurious. A private plane flew in lobsters from Boston for dinner. We set out on the quail shoot in mule-drawn carriages that had special places for the pointer dogs to sit. The terrain was flat and swampy with lots of cover. When the carriages could go no farther, we mounted well-trained quarter horses. The pointers were released by their handlers, and we followed them on horseback.

Suddenly, a dog would stand rigid and point. The host would assign two Guns to approach the covey of quail. The pointers would hold steady as the Guns approached. When the Guns were quite close to the dogs, the handlers would give a signal, and the dogs would jump at the covey. Generally, between eight and fifteen birds were in a covey. They would burst from cover with a sudden whirring of little wings. Each Gun would get to fire two shots. It was not difficult shooting, as the rising birds were not more than 20 yards away. The dogs would retrieve the dead birds, and we would continue forward on horseback.

We had a good barbecue in the field and ate the freshly shot quail with lobster salad and other delicacies. At dinner, we wore black tie, and afterward we played backgammon and bridge.

My visit to Seminole Plantation was a special shooting experience with charming people.

White-winged Doves in Mexico with Joe and Christina Hudson

I shot in Mexico only once, with good friends. I was in Houston, visiting Joe and Christina Hudson with Michel and Paul de Ganay. The Hudsons gave us a real Texas welcome, including a dove shoot in Mexico. We took their private plane to San Antonio and then drove south of the border. We stayed in a simple but very comfortable motel that had a swimming pool and Mexican food.

We surrounded a field where the doves would fly in to feed. The shooting was not difficult, but every Gun fired hundreds of cartridges.

The Mexicans were very friendly – there was lots of music and noise. I was told that Mexico City has about thirty million inhabitants, some of whom live in terrible poverty but are always friendly and hospitable. It is said that they have a traditional respect for ladies which dates from the time of the Spanish conquistadores.

In Texas we visited the Hudson ranch, which is quite close to that of former president George Bush. We saw Brahmin cattle, which have good resistance to the summer heat. All the buildings, even the stables, were air-conditioned, so when we stepped out of a building the heat really hit us. But nobody moved to Texas for the climate. Everyone wanted to find oil. There is plenty of oil in the state, but its exploitation is already well organized, and it's difficult to get good concessions to drill on.

We had a wonderful visit with the Hudsons, who later came to shoot with me in Spain and Scotland. Joe Hudson's mother, Titi Blaffer, married my good friend Prince Tassilo Furstenberg, who went to school with me in Vienna. Titi's father, Robert Blaffer, and his partner, William Farish, had drilled and found oil on the million-acre King Ranch in Texas and had started Humble Oil. I saw Titi Furstenberg regularly in Paris. She had lovely paintings and an indoor pool. Tassilo died a few years ago. His grandfather Prince Tassilo Festetics came from Keszthely and was the second-largest landowner in Hungary.

Mi-Voisin

The Sologne region, south of Orléans, encompasses a few hundred thousand acres. There are patches of woodland, and the ground is sandy – ideal for horseback riding. Traditionally, the Parisian bourgeoisie would shoot in this region. Claude Foussier had a nice property there, and so did many others who were kind enough to invite me. But the terrain was flat, so you did not have high-flying birds.

The 5000-acre shoot known as Mi-Voisin belonged to Marcel Bussac, a major industrialist who kept one of the finest racing stables in the world. He won the most prestigious races, including the Arc de Triomphe and the Derby at Epsom. When Marcel died, four brothers bought Mi-Voisin and decided to make a unique shoot there, but unfortunately they were businessmen, not sportsmen. I introduced them to the best gamekeepers in France, Trevor Housen, who had been with the British Special Air Services in the war, and his son-in-law Jim Hollyday. They did an outstanding job, but the owners did not give them a free hand, so after a few years, the shooting arrangements collapsed and the estate was sold.

Because these 5,000 acres were flat, I suggested that the new owners should create something there that would be rare in France, an outstanding shoot for grey partridges.

Elveden

I never shot at Elveden, but since my son-in-law Sebastian Guinness is a very enthusiastic Gun, I would like to write about this shoot, which his family came to own.

In the year 1086, a manor house at Elveden belonged to the abbot of Edmundsbury. After the dissolution of the monasteries by King Henry VIII, the manor passed through several families to the famous Admiral Viscount Keppel in 1768, and then to his nephew, the 4th Earl of Albemarle.

But it was the next owner, Maharaja Dhuleep Singh of Lahore, facetiously known as the "Black Prince", who became a giant in the history of shooting. He had been brought to England as a child, after the occupation of his state by British forces at the end of the Second Sikh War. The East India Company had confiscated from his family the famous Kohinoor Diamond, which was later presented to Queen Victoria, but the (British) Government of India had nonetheless granted him a generous privy purse. With these funds, Elveden was purchased for him by his trustees. The estate encompassed roughly 14,000 acres but produced very little income.

The maharaja came from a sporting background. His diverse interests included falconry, so he trained a number of Icelandic gyrfalcons to scoop up hares from the fields around Elveden. He also liked to shoot, and on September 8, 1876 the estate records indicate that His Highness killed 780 partridges by himself with only 1,000 shots.

Maharajah Dhuleep Singh

The day came when financial problems began to engulf the maharajah. His lavish entertainments could not be carried on indefinitely without income from his poorly managed estate, and his predicament eventually became desperate. When the (British) Government of India refused to increase his privy purse, the irate former ruler departed for Lahore, intent on starting a revolution in the Punjab. He was detained at Aden, however, and when the Russians refused to intervene for him, he moved to Paris and died there in 1893. He is buried at Elveden.

The maharaja's sons, Victor and Freddy, were also outstanding shots. On September 23, 1895, they bagged 846 partridges before lunch and then had to stop shooting because they were out of cartridges. The same year, on December 7th, the Guns at Elveden brought down 1,006 pheasants in 46 minutes.

The estate was eventually acquired by Edward Guinness, the principal heir to the Guinness brewing fortune who would soon become Viscount, and then Earl of, Iveagh. Guinness needed an appropriate place to entertain the society to which he had been admitted. So he purchased Elveden in 1894, and that year the game bag totaled 24,731 pieces, mainly pheasants, partridges, and hares. As the shoot's reputation grew, regular Guns came to include King Edward VII and the Prince of Wales (later King George V).

At Elveden, the shooting was extravagant. One entry in the estate records reads: "Wet weather, S.W. wind, five guns: His Majesty the King, Viscount Vallectort, the Hon. Sir Derek Keppel, the Hon. Henry Stonor, Viscount Iveagh (Edward Guinness): 1,122 cocks, 1,285 hens, 806 partridges, 18 hares, 13 rabbits, 4 various. Total: 3,248."

For shooting purposes, Elveden is currently divided. Approximately 10,000 acres belong to a Guinness family syndicate, 4,000 acres to a gun club that conducts rough shoots, and 3,000 acres to the Forestry Commission. There are presently six keepers and one trainer on the family shoot. At Elveden, shooting continues as an honored tradition and appears to be in good hands.

Biddick

This famous pheasant shoot at Chester-le-Street, near Durham, was one of the best and most popular in England. The owner, Tony Lambton, had renounced the earldom of Durham but was still addressed as Lord Lambton. He was one of the most accomplished shots of his day.

Line of Guns shooting high pheasants

Biddick encompassed about 30,000 acres. Lord Lambton's factor, Simon Grey, ran the shoot and normally rented it to Americans, among them Alfred Taubman, Henry Ford, and Jack Heinz. I shot there several times and can confirm that whoever gets the stand on the river, near the bridge, will experience some of the most challenging shooting in Britain. The kill would always be large – between 600 and 800 birds per day. "Bindie", Lady Lambton, was the charming and original hostess. Tony would shoot with his friends in January, when the quality of the birds would be outstanding. On commercial shoots, one doesn't dare to produce birds of such quality because the Guns can't hit them.

Helmsley

One can never say with certainty that a particular pheasant shoot is the best in Britain, but most of the best shots and proprietors of shoots would agree that Helmsley, in Yorkshire, is one of the best.

It was the 5th. Baron Feversham who established this estate as a major shoot, and it was managed, after his death in 1963, by my friend the shooting agent Colonel Kit Egerton. For a time, Helmsley was rented to Prince Stash Radziwill and Felix Fenston. When Fenston died, Lord Harry Ashcombe took his place, and after Radziwill's death, Harry had the whole shoot. He was kind enough to invite me to shoot there with lots of friends, including Ferdl Habsburg, "Bomps" Ratibor, Alex of Yugoslavia, Paul de Ganay, and others. We lodged in Helmsley at the Black Swan Hotel, where the food was superb.

On this shoot, the contour between the tops and bottoms of the dales is about 200 feet. The birds are driven from one ridge to the other, and the Guns are placed in the bottom of the dale. Some of the birds are definitely out of range, and in a strong wind you will have an extraordinary day, with everyone firing six or eight cartridges per bird.

Studley Royal

This superlative Yorkshire shoot was created by the 2nd. Marquess of Ripon, who is widely regarded as the greatest shot of all time. He also entertained the royalty and cream nobility of Europe. When he died in 1923, he had killed 556,813 game animals, from elephants to snipe.

In my time, Kit Egerton ran this shoot, and I shot there several times with my friend Claude Foussier. We averaged 350 to 500 birds per day, and some drives were top quality. The only problem was that the place was open to the public. A steady stream of tourists would drift in to look at the ruined monastery which had been burned down by King Henry VIII, and some of them would find themselves wandering among the Guns in the middle of a drive.

Luton Hoo Park

This estate in Bedfordshire was purchased by the diamond magnate and eventual knight Julius Wernher, who was originally from Germany. His son, Sir Harold, collected magnificent tapestries, paintings, and German silver. He married Countess Anastasia Mikhailovna, known as "Zia", a daughter of Grand Duke Michael of Russia, and imported to England her exquisite collection of Fabergé gold, jeweled, and enameled objects. Their daughter, Georgina, married Lieutenant-Colonel Harold ("Bunny") Phillips, who worked for British intelligence in Washington during World War II. He served as a contact between General Bill Donovan, who headed the American OSS, and his British counterpart, Bill Stevenson. One of Phillips's daughters married the Duke of Westminster, another the Duke of Abercorn; the only son, Nicky, was a trainee at Lazard Frères in Paris when I met him. Nicky married a charming girl from Central Europe named Lucie Czernin, also a friend of mine.

After his father's death, Nicky started a very ambitious real estate development business. We don't know precisely what happened, but financial problems closed in on him and caused this charming, intelligent, well-to-do young man to commit suicide. It was a terrible tragedy.

I visited his widow, Lucie, and tried to help her manage this 4,000-acre estate with its well-established shoot, all only 45 minutes from Claridges Hotel. But the shooting was stopped, the collections sold, and Lucie was left with only her two children.

I don't know what happened to Luton Hoo but am very grateful that I was able to shoot on this wonderful property.

Eastwell Manor

This country house in Kent belonged to H.R.H. Prince Alfred, Duke of Edinburgh, the second son of Queen Victoria. The duke left Eastwell Manor to his daughter, Princess Mary, who became Queen Marie of Romania and whose mother, Grand Duchess Maria, was the daughter of Czar Alexander II.

The house was refurbished, the gardens replanted, and there was a lake full of ducks in the park. The whole estate was quite impressive.

Eastwell Manor was bought for commercial shooting purposes. That it was close to both London and the Continent increased its popularity. Some of the pheasants flew well, and there was duck shooting, too. The bag depended on the demand and would sometimes total 800 pheasants per day. The American Guns wanted easier birds than the British and Continentals, as always.

One year, a tornado ruined the beautifully outlined drives and knocked down the ancient trees. The owner, a Mr. Bates, had to sell Eastwell Manor for very little.

Six Mile Bottom

Six Mile Bottom, near Newmarket, Suffolk, has an excellent pheasant shoot, but originally the plan was to shoot partridges there.

When General John Hall was shooting the estate, his theory was that the land was "quieter" in January, so he would shoot only then. Others would argue that partridge shooting should end by Christmas because partridges begin to pair after New Year's, and the best birds for shooting pair first. Also, the best partridge habitat should be shot over only once a year.

At Six Mile Bottom, September 25, 1930 was a remarkable day. The new owner, Capt. R.F.C. Cunningham-Reid, wanted to shoot a record bag of partridges, but in the first two drives only 50 birds were taken. The owner scolded the head keeper, and by the end of the day, the bag had risen to 1,418 partridges. With rabbits and hares thrown in, the total kill came to 1,499 pieces. No wonder that the most famous Guns, many of them royals, came to shoot at Six Mile Bottom.

Sadly, partridges began to disappear around 1960, and not just in England but on the Continent, due to the increasing use of artificial fertilizers that killed so many of the insects that the birds feed on. To run his shoot profitably, the owner turned to raising pheasants. The shoots were syndicated, with bags running at around 500 pheasants and some partridges.

I shot at Six Mile Bottom only once. Noel Cunningham-Reid gave us a memorable day, with everything professionally arranged. Luckily we had some wind. You need wind for the birds to fly well.

Crichel Downs

This lovely estate in Dorset belonged to Toby and Mariana Marten. They had a lovely manor house and were charming and hospitable hosts.

For years, I shot at Crichel Downs with more or less the same group of Guns with whom I had habitually hunted in Spain, Austria, and elsewhere in England. The estate was beautifully run, and the drives yielded plenty of pheasants. My friend Tom Troubridge had a cottage at Crichel Downs, and it was there that he shot the world record roebuck.

Thorp Perrow

While shooting in Yorkshire, I would lodge with Sir John Ropner in his lovely castle, Thorp Perrow, at Bedale. There were many good shoots thereabouts, and Sir John was also the best-known master-of-hounds in that region. His home was known for its arboretum. The food and service were always exquisite.

Thorp Perrow at Bedale, Yorkshire

At dinner, five waiters would serve us while the major domo stood watching in full dress. We would all be in black tie. Only the finest red and white wines would be served. After dinner, we would play gin rummy and backgammon over Monte Cristo No. 1 cigars. At Thorp Perrow, the other guests would often include President Valéry Giscard d'Estaing of France, Claude Foussier, Peter Payne, Élie de Rothschild, Gerald de Waldner, Claude Terrail, Olivier Dassault, and Robert Melinette.

Manderston House, Mellestrain, and Drumlanrig

Another place where I shot, often with the extraordinary Gun, Claude Foussier, was at Manderston House, in Berwickshire near Duns. This château dates from the nineteenth century and was owned by the 4th Baron Palmer. His wife, Cornelia, was charming and an excellent hostess.

Wilson Young had a shooting agency in that area, and it was there that he built up the famous drive known as "Long Walk," on the estate named Mellestrain, owned by the 12th Marquess of

Manderston House

Lothian. This is the only shoot where I saw pheasants zooming downhill so fast that they literally broke their wings. In this drive, every Gun fired over 200 cartridges, and some shot over 400. The pick-up men and their dogs would have to stand far behind the line of Guns, while we would bag between 300 and 500 pheasants.

Near Manderston House were other outstanding shoots. Alex and Aline Hays had one, and the Duke of Roxburghe had another. We shot with Lady McEwen at Marshmond and found it a nice property, but it was not developed for the quality of shooting we were looking for. The foregoing shoots were all in Berkwickshire, southeastern Scotland.

Claude Foussier and I also shot for several years at Drumlanrig, in Dumfriesshire, on a shoot belonging to the Duke of Buccleuch, but it had only two really good drives. We stayed with Giles Moncey-Haisham at Castletown, near Carlisle. He had some fine paintings of British navel vessels, as an ancestor of his had fought at Trafalgar.

Floors Castle

Guy Innes-Ker, 10th Duke of Roxburghe owned 50,000 acres around Kelso, in the Borders. His dukedom was created in 1707, and Floors Castle was built in 1721. Its park is spectacularly beautiful, and it is altogether special, inside and out. The duke also owned a very fine local hotel, where he had lived previously. He was a keen and excellent shot and had also served as chairman of the Scottish Wildlife Appeal. He would rent about twenty days of shooting to American, French, and British sportsmen. The shoot in his park was beautiful, and there were two excellent drives along the River Tees. On pheasant days, our bag would average 250 to 300 birds. It was well worthwhile to shoot there.

Floors Castle, Kelso, Roxburghshire, country seat of the dukes of Roxburghe

Chirk Castle and Sir Owen Watkin Williams Wynn

Among the many good shoots in rainy, hilly Wales, a few were special.

Alan Macintosh was already a friend of mine when he was a stockbroker in New York and was renting a house with Robin Wittgenstein on Gin Lane in Southampton. Alan had good contacts in Wales, and our group shot there, thanks to him.

Chirk Castle, where one of our shoots took place, has belonged to the Middleton family for centuries and dates back to the time when Wales was an independent country. The owner, David Middleton, had served as aide-de-camp to the 16th Earl of Dalhousie, when he was Governor-General of Rhodesia and Nyasaland.

At Chirk, there were two excellent drives with very high birds. Our group included Alan Macintosh and his charming wife, Jackie, their spaniel Charlie, Didi Kesselstatt, Peter Salm, Colin Campbell, and some extras. The bags were not too large – 300 to 350 birds. We stayed in an adequate hotel.

On one occasion, we drove past a large white house. The locals said that the Austrian consul lived there. Many years later, when our great friend Lisi Eltz, widowed Schönborn, married, we learned that the house belonged to her husband, Matthias Kaindl. I had hoped that Didi Kesselstatt would marry Lisi, but it didn't work out. Instead, she married Matthias, a very nice and well-to-do Austrian who also served as the honorary British consul in Salzburg. He has a wildlife park, where Ferdl Habsburg shot a stag with 17 kilos of antlers. Matthias is a successful businessman and a very good husband.

In Wales, I also shot with Sir Owen Watkin Williams Wynn. He had a unique drive where the pheasants were almost too high to be shot. Sir Owen is acclaimed for being the only known person to have served as master-of-hounds of two hunts at the same time – this due to his charm and popularity.

Milton's Exmoor Shoots, Ltd.

I was lucky enough to be invited for years on this very special shoot. Alan Milton was a Subaru car dealer who wanted to start a commercial shoot with only raised pheasants. I went and discussed the details with him. The shooting guests would be lodged at the little Royal Oak Hotel at Winsford, Devon, not far from Exmoor. This hotel was four or five hundred years old, and you had to watch your head when you passed through the low doorways. The guests would have to occupy the whole hotel, and hire the chef, who had previously run an excellent Chinese restaurant in Hong Kong.

I brought a group of my friends to Exmoor, and we were entirely satisfied with the shooting and accommodations. In Devon, you have extensive nivalations of up to 400 meters, and Alan Milton created drives there with bulldozers. The territory was not more than 2,000 acres, but Milton drove it every week, from mid-November on, as a three-day shoot. The bag was between 400 and 600 birds, and the Guns, who were mostly very fine shots, averaged six to eight cartridges for a bird.

The reputation of the shoot grew rapidly, and bookings had to be made one or two years in advance, as so many great Guns wanted to shoot there. Unfortunately, the cost of three days at Exmoor eventually became so exorbitant that I had to go elsewhere. Alan Milton was a good friend, but he became a rather expensive one.

These commercial shoots are ideal for the keen sportsman who does not have a first-class shoot of his own but wants to reciprocate invitations. You don't have to worry about anything; you just send a check.

The Espirito Santo Family

One reason I hunted in Angola and Mozambique with my brother, Paul, is that I have always been fond of Portugal and the Portuguese. Louise and I asked Nina Espirito-Santo to be the godmother of our daughter Peggy, who has for many years been friends with members of this lovely family. The Espirito-Santos own the largest private bank in Portugal, and from them I got letters of introduction to a number of government officials in Angola, which greatly facilitated our safari there.

The family also invited me to shoot partridges on their lovely estate at Comporta. I shot there with the Count of Barcelona, the father of the present King of Spain, and we greatly enjoyed reminiscing about how we had played footfall together at Lausanne in 1942. He was as charming as ever and shot beautifully.

The widow of István Horthy, Ily, with whom I danced in Vienna in 1937, married an amiable and interesting English officer, Colonel Guy Bowdon, who ran a travel agency in Estoril. Guy had been a military attaché in Baghdad with the British ambassador, our friend Sir Humphrey Trevelyan, when King Faisal was murdered and the political party of Saddam Hussein seized power. I bought from Colonel Bowdon fifty hectares of land, 12 kilometers from Lisbon, which was developed by my son, Peter, many years later.

Colonel Bowdon had a brother who lived in Nairobi. When the Mau Mau uprising broke out in 1952, many British settlers who had farmed in Kenya for decades sold or abandoned their estates. Bowdon's brother bought a number of large settler houses, speculating that when Kenya became independent, the major foreign governments would need large, impressive embassies. He was right.

Louise and I Hunt in Angola

My friend Jani Róth, whom I mentioned earlier, proceeded to make quite a lot of money. He had a friend in Angola, Sousa Machado, who owned a large open pit mine for iron ore at Tchamutete, not far from Luanda. The iron business was doing well in those days, for the Belgians and Japanese were buying the ore in any amount. So Jani got a few hundred Mercedes trucks and, with cheap African labor, exploited the mine and shipped the ore via Lobito and Luanda to anyone who would pay for it.

About that time, I decided to go to Angola on a safari, and Jani offered to make the arrangements for me. Louise came along, as she had never hunted in Africa. I warned her that I could not vouch for anything organized by Jani and that God only knew what would happen to us.

Unfortunately, we went in the wrong season. But we arrived with letters of introduction from our Portuguese banker friends, the Espirito-Santo family, to some of their factories and to some governors and army people. We visited Luanda, Lobito, and the southern part of Angola – all very interesting, but with limited hunting opportunities.

The Portuguese were very capable colonizers. Angola was not a colony but an integral part of Portugal, with Portuguese administration, police, post offices, and so on. Any native with a drop of white blood was considered white, but there was no racial discrimination of any kind. Angola was a very rich province that exported diamonds, coffee, iron ore, and agricultural products. Labor was cheap, and Portuguese industrialists had established all kinds of factories.

Safari in Mozambique with My Brother, Paul

Enchanted by life in Africa, where we had both hunted before, my brother Paul and I decided to go shooting in Mozambique, which was still an overseas province of Portugal, like Angola.

I arrived at Beira and met Paul, who had flown up from the capital, Lourenço Marques. The hunt started badly when an airline official could not locate my gun. I climbed into the hold of the plane and found it in a corner – hiding.

We had a splendid seafood luncheon at a restaurant owned by a Greek named George, who became our friend. In the afternoon, we met our white hunter, a sergeant in the Portuguese army. We learned right away that he knew very little about hunting, tracking, or trophies.

We had hoped to live in tents, with a big fire outdoors in the evenings, which would have created a safari atmosphere. Instead, we were housed afield in a small lodge with two bedrooms and a bath in between.

On the first day, I was fortunate enough to shoot a nyala, a member of the spiral-horned bushbuck family, like the kudu. It was to be my best trophy, and it still hangs over the fourteenth century fireplace of Duchess Anne of Clermont-Tonnerre in the Château de la Tour.

Because we had only one white hunter, we could normally hunt only one at a time. But once, when we saw three warthogs trotting along with their tails upright, we both grabbed our rifles and, after a flurry of shots, killed all three. The largest was a good trophy boar, and his head still hangs on a door in my home.

On one occasion, two buffaloes charged us. Paul and I waited until they got within 50 yards of our safari car. Then Paul shot one bull, and quite a good one, with his 8.64 caliber rifle. I shot the other one.

Back at Beira, we met our old friends François and Martine Edmond-Blanc. François had been president of the Conseil International de la Chasse and had more safari experience than anyone I know. I think he went on more than 120 big game hunts, worldwide, including shoots in Poland, Siberia, Mongolia, and Canada. Quite a number of his trophies can be seen in Paris at the Musée de la Chasse, at 60 rue des Archives.

More than the shooting, I simply enjoyed my brother's company on our hunt in Mozambique, and we both returned to Paris happy.

A Safari in Tanzania with Cousin Jay Mellon

In 1962, Uncle Matt Mellon invited Louise and me to accompany his son, James ("Jay"), on an African safari. This was to be a luxury expedition with two white hunters, African servants, and comfortable tented camps. The outfitter was Ker & Downey, the five-star firm that for many years had catered to sportsmen who were determined to live well while hunting for outstanding trophies. After our disappointing shoot in Angola, Louise and I were eager to go on an old-style safari with all the trimmings.

We flew to Nairobi, then continued in a single-engine plane to Seronera, in northern Tanzania. From there we set out across

Louise with her leopard, in Tanzania, 1962

My cape buffalo, in Tanzania, 1962

My record-class sable, taken in Tanzania, 1962

Cousin Jay Mellon with a greater kudu taken on our safari in Tanzania, 1962

the vast, treeless Serengeti Plains by Land Rover and eventually entered a blackened region of freshly burned grassland with scattered acacia trees. This was the Maswa hunting area, where Ker & Downey had pitched a camp for us. Cousin Jay had already arrived from Kenya.

For several days we hunted for lion, leopard, buffalo, and plains game. On one occasion, I had to pursue a wounded lion into dense underbrush before finishing him off. I also shot a good buffalo with 43 inches of horn and collected a number of plains antelope, including the graceful impala.

We then journeyed deep into central Tanzania and camped on the Great Ruaha River, 85 miles south of Dodoma. There, in a landscape of arid mountains covered with tangled thorn bush, we hunted for greater kudu. Jay shot an exceptional kudu bull with over 60 inches of horn, and Louise killed a leopard, which we baited in typical fashion by suspending an antelope carcass in an acacia tree.

We then moved camp to the Rungwa River, a day's drive to the southwest. There the terrain consisted of open woodland, where we normally had 200 yards of visibility between the trees. Tsetse flies were a nuisance, and we had to shoo them away from our faces continually. Sable and roan antelope were the most sought-after trophies in that region, and we collected fine heads of both. I shot a record-class sable with over 41 inches of horn, and Jay scored with a record 29-inch roan. I also bagged a fine bull eland, and Jay shot a 40-inch sable.

Louise and I had to leave the safari early to attend my brother-in-law Billy Hitchcock's wedding, but we had shot a number of superior trophies, some of which still hang on our walls.

Red Deer in the Mármaros

This lovely region is in White Russia, where Hungary, Romania, Poland, and Slovakia converge. It belonged to Hungary until World War I but is now part of Slovakia. It is mountainous, and small rivers descend to the Hungarian Plateau. In 1939, this region briefly reverted to Hungary, and my father rented a lovely

Gold medal red deer stag

shoot there, with deep lakes full of trout, and bears, wolves, lynx, and very fine red deer stags in the woods.

With my friend Vincent Szakall, his good-looking sister, Mária, and my cousin Elvira Stephaich, I visited this area to shoot a trophy stag.

There were two very small lodges where we would stay at night. I had a motor bike, which I took with me for shopping. We had two local gamekeepers who knew nothing about game. But the weather was beautiful and the company excellent.

It was the mating season, and when we heard a stag roaring, we would just set out through the woods to stalk him – there were no forest tracks or trails. I eventually shot a fine old sixteen-pointer with seven kilos of horn. We were blissfully happy to have spent ten days there.

I Attempt to Revive Bird Shooting
In Post-Communist Hungary

It was through my friend Colonel Kit Egerton that I met a young gentleman, about thirty years old, named Christopher Robinson. He had served in a well-known British cavalry regiment and was a keen sportsman. His passions were shooting and fishing.

When communism miraculously ended in Hungary without a shot being fired, I suggested to Robinson that we attempt to organize pheasant shooting there, but only with birds that would fly well. Hungary had always been renowned for its wonderful shoots, the people were accustomed to hunting, and I was convinced that this tradition could be revived there at a lower cost than in most of the other European countries.

I talked with the first non-Communist Prime Minister, József Antall. I had known his father, who had been in charge of refugees after the brief German-Polish War of 1939. The elder Mr. Antall had collaborated with my father and Monsignor Béla Varga to establish schools for Polish refugees and had unofficially helped Poles to escape through Hungary to Austria, Italy, and

North Africa or to join the Free Polish forces under General Wladyslaw Sikorski.

I explained to the prime minister that organized shooting could bring the country some much-needed foreign currency. He introduced me to the minister of agriculture, who passed me down to an assistant, who passed me farther down to a junior employee of the Ministry. I asked this young man what experience he had in shooting, and he replied, "No experience, sir." So nothing came of my effort to organize state-sponsored shooting in Hungary, though all the essentials were there: good territory, good shooting personnel, and confiscated castles in which to lodge the Guns.

Again, I contacted Prime Minister Antall. This time, he gave his blessing to our venture. Southeastern Hungary, near the Romanian border, had always been famed for its shooting. The Almásy, Wenckheim, and Tisza families had owned large estates with outstanding shoots there. I contacted two Hungarians who came from there and were well connected locally for shooting.

During the Communist regime, 1948 to 1989, all land belonged to the state. The government had created state farms on the Soviet model, and the shooting rights were allocated to hunting societies, which paid rent to these farms. My two representatives went from one hunting society to the next, explaining that foreigners wanted to rent two or three days of shooting and would pay in foreign currency. The hunting societies were delighted to receive the money, which we paid in German marks. With these funds they could pay the keepers and buy feed for the pheasants, and so on.

One hunting society had the shooting rights for 5,000 to 15,000 hectares. By renting three to five days of shooting to us, the members were able to shoot during the season themselves and still have money left over. The societies had thirty to sixty members, so half of them would beat the game toward the other half. The next weekend they reversed the order, so that everyone had a chance to shoot.

We needed forty to sixty beaters, loaders, picker-ups, and porters. We also needed lodging for the Guns – a place where simple Hungarian food and good wines would be available. What we got was quite different. We offered to advance twenty-five percent of the rental fee to feed the existing pheasants, to buy more pheasants for breeding, to repair the cars, and to buy whatever else was required for a successful shoot. The societies accepted the money but used it for their own purposes. We had counted on shooting 400 to 500 birds per day with eight Guns, and we were prepared to pay in German marks for every bird. But to shoot this number of birds, you have to release twice as many, and the societies would not use the advanced money to do this. Instead, they spent the advance on whatever they wanted. We bagged only 150 to 200 birds per day, and since the Guns had counted on more than twice that number, they were sorely disappointed.

I had to explain all of this to Christopher Robinson. The Guns ended up being charged for only 150 to 200 birds per day, but everyone agreed that it was not worth coming from London, Paris, or New York to shoot so few birds. With the hotel and food we had no problem. There was always plenty of goose liver and other Hungarian delicacies, which the foreigners enjoyed.

After three years of trying to convince the hunting societies to deliver what they had promised in the contract, we had to give up and close down our operation. Morale was very low in Hungary after forty years of Communist misrule and Soviet occupation, hence the crooked behavior that we experienced.

Baronscourt

The owner, Jamie Hamilton, now Duke of Abercorn, had organized his first shoot for paying guests, and I was invited to participate. The castle, the garden, and the estate were excellent, but the organization was inexperienced and the quality of the pheasants was not what we had hoped for. That said, the quality of the host and hostess compensated for that of the birds.

Crom Castle

This eminently comfortable castle belongs to the 6th Earl Erne – "Harry" to his friends – who is married to Anna Bjorck, a Swedish beauty who had been the wife of Louise's cousin Center Hitchcock.

We hunted in the bogs and shot some very sporty snipe. We also made two drives for pheasants. At Crom, the atmosphere was charming – lots of whisky and a very amusing group. Harry and Anna were perfect hosts. I left with lovely memories.

Sierndorf

I did not shoot many pheasants in Austria, but I do remember one shoot given by Count Rudi Colloredo-Mannsfeld at Sierndorf, not far from Vienna.

This shoot had a familiar flaw: too many aristocrats and not enough pheasants. But I hasten to add that the 250 birds that we shot flew well and that the Guns were all charming gentlemen.

Whoever wrote the shooting list did so alphabetically so that no one would be offended. There were eight Guns, all with well-known historical names, such as Schönborn, Széchenyi, Seilern, Ratibor, Mayr-Melnhof, and Pantz.

We dined in a fourteenth-century castle with lovely little countesses and fabulous wines and champagne. As always, the company was more important than the number of birds, though it is certainly best to have both.

Shooting with Count Holstein in Denmark

Lajos Károlyi organized this pheasant shoot. For safety reasons, to shoot with more than one shotgun was prohibited in Denmark, but we were given a picker-up with a well-trained retriever. During the drive, our dog began to howl and ran away. I looked back and saw my picker-up lying on the ground. His face was dark blue. The poor fellow had had a heart attack, and he died en route to the hospital. We wanted to cancel the shoot, but Count Holstein's son insisted that we continue. It's always interesting to shoot in a new place. In this case, we came to realize how spoiled we were. On the other hand, Count Holstein had seven daughters, who graciously waited on us at lunch.

Aalhom Castle

Alfred Taubman's rental of Aalhom Castle in Denmark was arranged by Prince Michel of Bourbon-Parma. Someone then canceled, and Michel invited me. There were plenty of pheasants, but they did not fly very well and the organization was faulty. I nonetheless enjoyed myself, because my friend François de Riocour was there. We shot about 600 birds. The castle was okay.

Commercial Shoots in France

Every year, 1.5 million shooting licenses were issued in France, but there were very few good private shoots. The owners of the best ones would shoot on each other's estates, but a man who had no estate of his own and could not offer reciprocal shooting might have to make other arrangements. For him a favorable alternative would be to rent one or another of the purely commercial shoots. Three of them were excellent, and all were located just outside Paris:

(1) Dampierre

This beautiful property, with its outstanding château, belongs to Jean d'Albert, Duke of Luynes and Chevreuze. If you own a historic castle of this size and quality, it costs you a fortune to maintain. The only two ways to make money on such a property are (1) to take in paying guests, as in a luxury hotel, or (2) to make a good shoot.

Jean turned Dampierre into the foremost commercial shoot in France. He also created a gourmet restaurant in his former stables. His château has a 400-acre park surrounded by a wall, and Jean breeds some pheasants and duck there, but he also buys birds when he needs them. The shoot is run with perfect efficiency. You can tell the host how many birds you want to shoot, and everything will be ready for you, including an excellent lunch in the château with the charming duchess, who is also an accomplished shot. Her father is my friend Henri Roussel, one of the great international Guns. Roussel founded a famous game park in Kenya, which he sold to Adnan Kashoggi and Alec Wildenstein.

I think that Jean de Luynes is today the best living shot in France. He frequents the leading shoots in his own country but also those in England and Spain. I feel lucky to have shot at Dampierre a few times as the guest of some generous friends who bought a day's shooting and then invited their favorite shooting companions. Dampierre was so close to Paris that by 6:00 P.M., the guests would be back at the Hotel Ritz and in their baths.

PHEASANTS			
PLACE	DATE	HOME OF	TOTAL
Hall Barn (Bucks)	18 Dec. 1913	Lord Burnham	3,937
Warter Priory (Yorks)	5 Dec. 1909	Lord Nunburnholme	3,824
Sandringham (Norfolk)	4 Nov. 1896	Prince of Wales	3,114
Tot Magyar (Hungary)	10 Dec. 1909	Count Karolyi	6,125

PARTRIDGES			
Holkham (Norfolk)	7 Dec. 1905	Lord Leicester	1,671
Welbeck (Notts)	10 Oct. 1906	Duke of Portland	1,504
The Grange, Alresford (Hants)	4 Nov. 1897	Lord Ashburton	1,461
Sandringham (Norfolk)	10 Nov. 1905	Prince of Wales	1,342
St. Johann (Hungary)	1892?	Baron Hirsch	2,870

RED GROUSE			
Littledale (Lancs)	12 Aug. 1915	Lord Sefton	2,929
Broomhead (Yorks)	27 Aug. 1913	R. H. Rimington-Wilson	2,843
Broomhead (Yorks)	24 Aug. 1904	R. H. Rimington-Wilson	2,748
Roan Fell (Scotland)	30 Aug. 1911	Duke of Buccleuch	2,523

RABBITS			
Blenheim (Oxon)	7 Oct. 1898	Duke of Marlborough	6,943
Rhinlas (Wales)	1885	Mr. Lloyd Price	5,086

HARES			
Holkham (Norfolk)	19 Dec. 1977	Lord Leicester	1,215

SHOOTING ALONE			
PLACE	DATE	PERSON	TOTAL
Elveden (Suffolk)	8 Sept. 1876	Maharajah Duleep Singh	780 Partridges
Bluberhouses (Yorks)	30 Aug. 1888	Lord Walsingham	1,070 Grouse
Wemmergill (Yorks)	20 Aug. 1872	Sir Fred. Milbank	190 Grouse (1 Drive)
St Johann (Hungary)	1893	Lord de Grey	240 Partridges (1 Drive)
Grandtully (Scotland)	12 Aug. 1871	Maharajah Duleep Singh	440 Grouse (Over Dogs)
Hunt Hill (Scotland)	14 Aug. 1887	Captain Tomasson	458 Grouse (Over Dogs)

Record bags of birds, rabbits, and hares

(2) Voisin

Near Rambouillet and not more than an hour from Paris, the noted banker Count Christian de Fels created the commercial shoot known as Voisin. Its terrain was not particularly beautiful, and the château dated only from the nineteenth century, but Christian was an excellent host, and almost everyone who counted in the shooting world would frequent either his shoot or Dampierre. The English were the exception. With their superb natural pheasant shoots, they would not go to France unless they were invited to some special event where they could spend an agreeable day with friends. They preferred shooting "at home", on their beloved island.

3) Marolles

This property belonged to Henri Couturier and had some very nice drives. It was rented by François Péreire and Baron Alain de Gunzburg. Bankers like P. L. Dreyfus and Jean-Marc Vernes used to shoot there. The tableau would be around 500 birds – all pheasants and ducks.

Shooting Records

Frankly, I am not fond of shooting to break records, but it is an interesting subject. We read that the ancient Egyptian sportsmen seldom used bows or slings but instead "throw-sticks". The fallen game was collected by attendants, who then presented a fresh "stick" to the sportsman. This was in the 8th and 9th dynasties, 1580 to 1320 B.C.

What is believed to be the first mention of firearms being used to hunt game occurs in a book written by Emperor Maximilian in 1504. Though modern firearms for hunting were not invented until long after that date, they have not changed much in the last hundred years.

Fortunately, many recent shooting records have survived, so I will try to come up with some figures for the last century and earlier.

Pheasants

Originally from China, this bird was a favorite dinner dish in ancient Rome, and it is widespread in Europe and America today. Having written extensively about pheasant hunting, I will now concentrate on record bags.

Everyone agrees that the world record for pheasants was set on the Károlyi family's estate, Tót-Megyer, in northwestern Hungary, where 6,125 completely wild birds were killed in one day, along with 150 hares and 50 partridges. I wrote about this shoot earlier.

Exceptionally large pheasant kills were also made by the Earl of Derby at Knowsley, by the Duke of Portland at Welbeck, by Lord Hill at Hawston, by Lord Iveagh at Elveden, by Lord Ashburton at Buckenham, and by Lord Sefton at Croxteth. The bag on these shoots and at Hall Barn, Beaconsfield, and Warter Priory was normally more than 2,500 birds per day, and the number of Guns was normally limited to eight.

Just to name-drop, here are some of the most accomplished shots between 1890 and 1910: King Edward VII, the Prince of Wales (later King George V), Maharajah Dhuleep Singh (the "Black Prince"), Lord Ripon, Lord Walsingham, Lord Ilchester, Lord Dalhousie, Lord Herbert Vane-Tempest, the Hon. Henry Stonor, Lord Lovat, the Duke of Roxburghe, Lord Manners, and others.

In recent times, the finest pheasant shoots would include Gurston Down, Studley Royal, Dallowgill, Helmsley, Biddick, and Garrowby.

Grey Partridges

The British one-day record for partridges – 1,671 birds, taken on November 7, 1905 – was set on the 2,000-acre Holkham estate in Norfolk, but I think this record has since been broken by Sir Joe Nickerson in Lincolnshire, where he is said to have brought down 2,000 birds with six Guns. In the records for partridges, we find again the names of the immortal shots, Maharajah Dhuleep Singh, Colonel Willoughby, and Lord Coke, among others.

It is also recorded that in 1906, the Duke of Portland's party shot 1,478 partridges at Welbeck Abbey. Partridge driving in Scotland did not compare with its English counterpart. In Scotland, a bag of 400 birds in a day was very good.

In France, partridge shooting could be excellent. In September 1898, on the plains of Beauce, between Orléans and Chartres, twenty Guns killed 3,000 birds in two days. Chantilly, the shoot of the princes of Condé, was also excellent.

Red-legged Partridges

We know that King Charles I of England imported red-legged partridges from France in the seventeenth century and that Lords Hertford and Rochford imported the birds in larger numbers around 1777. In England, no one is known to have shot 1,000 of these birds in a day. Hunters fared better in Spain, where up to 3,000 birds a day have been taken with twelve to fourteen Guns.

During forty years of shooting red-legged partridges in Spain, I was fortunate to have experienced some extraordinary shoots in that country, some of which I have described. Pepe Ramón Mora-Figueroa, Juanito Abeillo, and Count Bunting de Teba, an ancestral nephew of Empress Eugénie of France, are probably the best Spanish Guns to date, and it was an honor to have shot with them. The Marquis Carlos de Paul and the brothers Carlos and Pepe March are also still first-class shots. No one can beat the Spaniards at partridge shooting, nor the English at shooting high, fast-flying pheasants.

Driven partridges

So many of the pheasants and partridges one shoots nowadays are raised and released. In January, the raised partridges fly better than at other times, but they never fly as well as wild birds. It is also unfortunate that most of the red-legged partridge shoots in Spain are now commercial. Not many people can afford to shoot 1,000 birds at $70 a bird.

Black Grouse

In Dumfriesshire, Scotland, 247 of these birds were killed by ten Guns, on October 4, 1869, and large bags were being shot on other estates as well.

Red Grouse

The record bag of red grouse was obtained on the "Glorious Twelfth" of August, 1915, on the Littledale and Abbeystead beats by eight Guns, who included the Earl of Sefton, the Hon. J. Ward, the Hon. H. Stonor, Major the Hon. J. Dawnay, and others. There were six drives, and the final tally of red grouse came to 2,929 – over 360 birds per Gun.

On August 27, 1913, nine Guns shooting on Broomhead Moor, Yorkshire, took 2,843 grouse, and in 1893, the tally for one day came to 2,648. It is interesting that this moor, which covered only 4,000 acres, would produce 5,000 grouse in a season. In those days, a good day of driving occasionally yielded 700 birds. If you compare these figures with those of today, you have to admit that something has gone wrong.

The greatest number of grouse killed by a single Gun in one day is still 1,070. This was done by the 6th. Earl of Walsingham on his Blubberhouse Moor, in Yorkshire, on August 30, 1888. The first drive began at 5:12 A.M. and the walk home was at 7:30

P.M. Using a pair of Purdey hammer-guns, Lord Walsingham fired 1,510 cartridges, including 40 signal shots not fired at birds. People would say, "You must have been dead tired!" and the earl would reply, "Not at all! Though I was shooting black powder all day, I played cards till midnight, as always."

Sir Frederick Milbank averaged 728 grouse a day at Wemmergill, Yorkshire, where his record for one drive was 190.

Sand Grouse

Sand grouse are very numerous in many parts of Africa and India. I shot a few in Tanzania. They would fly in to a waterhole between 7:30 and 9:00 A.M., and an hour later, they would all be gone.

It is recorded that at Bikaner, India, 3,532 sand grouse were shot in one day by an unknown number of Guns. Of these, the maharajah shot 466 himself.

Quail

Quail are relatively rare in England but remain numerous along the Mediterranean coasts. They are migratory and fly north in April and May. The island of Capri was famous for a thousand years as a seasonal haven for migrating quail, but they were netted in large numbers, then sold and eaten. Egypt is still famous for quail shooting, and so is Spain, where the record for one day is 980. In Central Europe, quail have become rare, in part because of the widespread use of chemicals for fertilizing the fields.

Capercaillie

This species became extinct in Scotland around 1762 and in Ireland maybe two years earlier. The largest of all grouse, this bird was reintroduced from Sweden between 1827 and '37, and it is recorded that on November 4, 1910, sixty-nine capercaillies were taken in Scotland by seven Guns, all from the local aristocracy and gentry.

Woodcock

Ireland claims the record kill for woodcock – 228 birds shot by six Guns at Ballykine, County Galway. In 1877, the Marquess of Hamilton killed 342 woodcock at Baronscourt, in County Tyrone, with a party of three to five Guns.

Woodcock

Woodcock join in large-scale migrations. Fair Isle, situated between the Orkney and Shetland Islands, was a stopover for large numbers of these birds during their seasonal migrations. The birdwatcher George Stout claims to have shot 109 woodcock with a 410 shotgun on Fair Isle in 1908.

I have an old friend, Count Mark Pejacsevich, still living, whose father owned 100,000 acres in Croatia, with 10,000 acres of fish ponds, and his estate was directly on the migratory route that the woodcock followed on their annual flight to Albania and the Greek islands.

I remember that woodcock hunters always tried to shoot the number of the year in birds. So in 1936, they tried to shoot that number of woodcock. I also recall that anyone who shot 500 woodcock in his lifetime at Nasice, in Croatia, would receive a gold tie pin with a woodcock head on it. One hunter, Tom Purdey, of shotgun renown, killed 1,000 woodcock at Nasice and was awarded a tie pin with a woodcock head made of diamonds. Years later, at a cocktail party, a friend of mine saw a gentleman with a diamond woodcock head on his tie pin. He said to the man, "You are Tom Purdey." Astonished, Tom asked how my friend had recognized him. My friend replied, "Because it was my father who gave you that tie pin."

Snipe

Large bags of snipe were formerly taken in Ireland and on the Inner Hebrides. In olden times, when the land was not as scientifically farmed, there was also good snipe shooting in England. Bags of 100 to 150 birds, driven to Guns or walked up, have been recorded. Snipe were also formerly common in Normandy, parts of Algeria, India, and Albania.

I have shot snipe in Ireland on the estate of my old friend Lord Harry Erne. We walked them up, and with four or five Guns we would shoot 15 or 20 in one morning. In Anglaisy, in northern Wales, my friend Mark Pejacsevich and I drove and walked up snipe with superbly trained spaniel dogs, but we never shot more than 20 birds in a day.

I never shot snipe in Normandy, but my friends Jacques Firmen-Didot, Charles de Ganay, Marc Henrion, and others did hunt there and obtained bags of 20 to 25 birds, but not more. Driving snipe or walking them up in the bogs is good sport. They fly fast and call for a quick shot.

Mallard Ducks

Nowadays, it is easy and very common to raise mallards artificially. Often, it is also quite difficult to distinguish between true wild birds and those that have been raised for release.

In England, sportsmen normally distinguish between the different kinds of ducks. Teal, widgeon, shoveler, pochard, tufted, and pintail are counted separately in the daily bag. On the Continent, with the occasional exception of teal, the different species are generally lumped together as simply "ducks".

In Europe, the three principal reserves for waterfowl are the deltas of the Nile, Danube, and Guadalquivir rivers. While shooting is now prohibited in all of these areas, I was lucky enough to have shot in the Nile Delta fifty years ago, as previously described, and I visited the other two areas without a gun.

As I wrote earlier, my Egyptian friend Manolo Vafiades shot from a butt next to mine more than 500 waterfowl in the Nile Delta between 7 A.M. and 1 P.M. He was shooting with two automatic guns while sitting in a barrel. He did not know what kinds of ducks he was shooting, but his final count did not include any of the other water birds, such as pelicans, storks, or ibises. I also recall that near Cairo, my friend Peter Stirling shot over 400 ducks in a morning on the lakes near the British

Embassy. And not so long ago, my friends Kiko Bemberg and André de Ganay shot 250 ducks per gun in one morning in the delta of the Guadalquivir.

In France, there were two very good lakes for ducks: one in the Brenne region, belonging to George and Jacqueline Vernes, the other to Jean-Pierre and Christiane Guerlain, at Grand Lieu. I never shot in either place, but I understand that there were never more than four Guns and that during the migration, each Gun shot 100 birds a day. At Henri Roussel's shoot in the Sologne, over 1,000 ducks were shot by eight Guns in a single hour, but they were all released birds.

I have lovely memories of shooting released mallards on Peter Salm's shoot at Southampton, New York, but we never shot more than 15 birds per Gun. There were many places where four or five Guns would bag 1,000 ducks, in a few hours. Archduke Franz Ferdinand of Austria-Hungary had a shoot where the daily bag per Gun was frequently over 300 ducks.

I must also mention that my friend Dudás Nagy, a great authority on waterfowl shooting, still shoots ducks in Chile, at the age of a hundred. That is also a kind of record!

Mallard ducks are easy to raise, and it's fun to shoot a hundred of them between pheasant drives.

Geese

I do not intend to write about the different kinds of geese – Canada, barnacle, grey-legged, pink-footed, and brant, among others. There appear to have been very few people who have shot over 200 wild geese per day, whether in Spain, Canada, India, Africa, Argentina, or America. In Hungary, on the lakes of Count Tisza, in Geszt, three Guns – Duke Albrecht of Bavaria, Count

László Szápáry, and Count Dudás Nagy – shot 286 geese, but none of them was able to shoot 100. The next day Szápáry, who was an excellent shot, bagged 208 geese and 65 ducks, setting the all-time record for one Gun in Hungary.

On Bill Stirling's estate in Scotland, between 15,000 and 25,000 geese would occasionally spend the night on the Ardoch lochs. Their morning flight out and evening return were unique spectacles. But none of us ever bagged 100 geese in one day.

Wood Pigeons

A total of 467 wood pigeons are known to have been killed in Britain by Cecil FitzHerbert. The game laws of various countries favor the shooting of these birds, because they are so harmful to agriculture. In the years between 1960 and 1980, Archie Cootes made a profession out of shooting wood pigeons and would often bag over 400 a day. Accompanied by a retriever, he would go from farm to farm shooting the birds for a fee. I have never been able to find out why these pigeons are so numerous.

In southern France, to which the birds migrate in large numbers from Africa, pigeon shooting is very popular.

I spent some lovely days in Banffshire, shooting pigeons with my friend Lord Seafield, and I remember that on one occasion, when there was a big wind, I shot nearly 100 birds in two hours.

Turtle Doves

These doves are also migratory. They fly twice a day: once in the morning when going from their roosting places to feed, and again in the afternoon, when they return.

For ten years, I would shoot turtle doves at Tarudan, near Agadir, Morocco, where we always lodged at the luxurious

Shooting wood pigeons

Hotel Gazelle d'Or. We always had wonderful sport there, but I must add that a Spanish friend of mine shot over 2,000 of these doves per day by himself near Córdoba, Argentina. He used four 410-gauge automatics and would fire over 3,000 cartridges.

There were also large numbers of these birds in Colombia, but owing to the political situation, few people go there to shoot at present. I highly recommend going to Argentina, where one fires 500 to 1000 cartridges a day. The birds fly fast there, and the shooting can be described only as wonderful sport.

Hares

There are several shoots in England where 1,000 hares have been taken in one day, but bags of twice that number were shot in Hungary, Bohemia, and elsewhere in Central Europe. Unlike rabbits, which build their warrens in thickets, hares prefer the open fields, so a great deal of their habitat has been destroyed by agriculture. Like the grey partridge, they have become rare all over Europe.

Rabbits

On the ducal estate of Blenheim, 6,943 rabbits, 26 hares, and 13 partridges were killed on October 7, 1898 by five Guns: the Duke of Marlborough, Princes Victor and Freddy Singh (the sons of Maharajah Dhuleep Singh), Sir Robert Gresley, and Mrs. Stephen Wombwell. The shooting began at 9:10 A.M. and stopped at 5:40 P.M., minus 35 minutes for lunch. There were seven drives.

As children, we had lots of fun shooting rabbits by using ferrets to drive them from their holes. The disease known as myxomatosis, which was invented by a French doctor, decimated the rabbit populations in Europe and the British Isles. An infected rabbit was smuggled into Australia and started the epidemic there, to the delight of the local farmers.

Remarkable Shots

There is an old Hungarian saying that everyone lies before an election, when getting married, and after shooting or fishing. During the nineteenth century, the ratio between birds killed and cartridges fired was about 41 to 59. But this is an overall figure. It does not take into account how the birds were flying or other important variables. Lord Ripon and Lord Walsingham, probably the two best shots of the late nineteenth and early twentieth centuries, said that a man might consider himself a good shot if he killed 30 percent of the birds he shot at, but they were probably assuming that the hypothetical shot was a sportsman, like they were, and would pass up many of the easiest birds. It may be recorded that So-and-So shot 35 grouse with the same number of cartridges or 65 pheasants straight, but his total will be vastly less impressive if he refused to pass up easy birds. Grouse shot against a strong wind are hardly moving, and pheasants that are raised and released or walked up with dogs are hardly sporting to shoot.

Another problem in evaluating shooting ability arises from the scarcity of records. I am not aware that we have anything like complete figures for Archduke Franz Ferdinand, Count Czernin, Count Draskovich, Sr., and others from Central Europe, because many of the hunting records and related literature disappeared during and after the two world wars. Only the British and Spanish records are reasonably complete. That said, I will try to give a résumé that should be reasonably authoritative.

In 1887, Sir Ralph Payne-Gallwey, a knowledgeable Gun of the late nineteenth century, selected the following as the best shots of his day:

The 6th Earl of Walsingham

The 2nd. Marquess of Ripon
The 6th. Earl of Walsingham
The 10th. Earl of Southesk
The 4th. Earl of Carnarvon
The 4th. Baron Ashburton
Sir Frederick Millbank
The Hon. Henry Stonor
Maharajah Dhuleep Singh

Lord Walsingham killed over 70.8 percent of the birds he shot at when he bagged 1,070 driven partridges on his Blubberhouse Moor, in Yorkshire, on August 30, 1888, and Maharajah Dhuleep Singh killed 78.9 percent of the birds he shot at when he alone bagged 780 partridges.

In the late nineteenth century, people were already competing in live pigeon and glass ball shoots, the forerunners of today's skeet and trap competitions. It is recorded that a certain Captain Bogardus shot 500 live pigeons in 8 hours and 48 minutes, and that in December 1879 he broke 5,500 glass balls in 7 hours and 20 minutes.

In my youth, I used to shoot glass balls thrown out of a machine, and I remember that after a while I did not miss many – or any.

It is also recorded that at Sandringham, the 2nd. Marquess of Ripon shot 28 pheasants in one minute, timed by a friend with a stopwatch.

Early in the twentieth century, Lord Alvenley and Lord de Ros were out shooting together and agreed that each should carry whatever the other shot. Lord Alvenley, who was a practical joker, shot a donkey. How Lord de Ros got out of this bargain is not known.

I remember making a bet with François de Riocour about who could break the most clay pigeons with 1,000 cartridges. I was

The 2nd Marquess of Ripon taking a high bird

given a handicap of ten, because he was the better shot. François broke 820 clays, but I was never able to break more than 800. We then made a bet about how long it would take each of us to fire 1,000 cartridges at these clays. In both contests, the clays were easy to hit, as they came from the same trap. We had someone to massage our left arms when we got tired. It took us about one hour

GAME KILLED BY THE 2ND MARQUESS OF RIPON FROM 1867 TO 1923

	Rhinoceros	Tiger	Buffalo	Sambur	Pig	Deer	Red Deer	Grouse	Partridges	Pheasants	Woodcock	Snipe	Wild Duck	Black Game	Capercailzie	Hares	Rabbits	Various	Total
1867							8	265	1179	741	20	22	10			719	934	115	4013
1868							35	201	1418	1601	28	67	23			690	543	113	4719
1869							35	135	1659	1431	26	133	37			547	443	122	4568
1870							21	498	2309	2117	36	53	30			833	626	137	6660
1871							55	1408	1598	1859	80	244	42			1093	341	225	6945
1872							38	1498	2083	2835	27	60	31			1108	756	235	8671
1873							25	248	2417	3050	95	263	85			1027	450	591	8251
1874						3	5	90	2878	2345	229	462	131	5	4	1200	302	1200	8854
1875							3	287	2882	3225	176	461	208			1376	576	743	9937
1876							3	1551	3394	4110	30	25	37			1245	890	266	11,551
1877						2	4	2032	2359	4235	35	45	33	11	11	1496	1044	309	11,616
1878						4	9	1669	3378	4679	43	44	55	5	6	2157	662	503	13,214
1879							4	1344	630	3140	132	92	62	9	11	1125	287	215	7051
1880	9	6	18	31	73	12		1131	682	531	9	47	54	26	5	501	141	408	3684
1881							5	1566	3465	5014	26	14	43			1058	791	166	12,148
1882	2	2	6	1	66	104	10	3025	2123	2370	14	21	44			464	1122	117	9491
1883							5	2896	1845	6119	157	84	155			918	1386	319	13,884
1884							10	3073	3523	4347	134	70	70			713	1896	453	14,289
1885							5	2015	2788	4620	104	23	31			589	2547	108	12,830
1886							20	1989	1463	3383	105	87	72			357	786	349	8611
1887							57	2258	3785	3387	104	3	12			415	2328	237	12,586
1888							4	3060	853	5072	31	151	10			307	1523	83	11,096
1889							5	3081	5751	6182	100	109	14	38	8	1747	1069	135	18,239
1890								2006	7002	6498	172	105	28			1446	1120	123	18,500
1891								2277	1699	5794	34	13				711	406	271	11,205
1892							1	1412	6784	5580	7	10	5			453	1233	281	15,766
1893								2611	8732	5760	66	7	42			837	914	166	19,135
1894							1	2567	7261	5034	76	7	12			935	580	222	16,695
1895							1	1272	3461	6101	11	13	17			352	1040	210	12,478
1896								2649	2613	8514	13	11	4			314	557	177	14,852
1897							1	2797	1914	7850	67	10	47			358	828	152	14,024
1898								1693	1200	3432	18	3	6			169	298	144	6963
1899								823	1309	4605	16	2	57			205	609	137	7763
1900								1033	1322	6762	24	8	95			223	819	141	10,427
1901								2037	1991	8478	8	11	141			262	595	114	13,637
1902								1706	1701	4998	11	3	166			268	479	280	9612
1903								1890	462	4709	16	3	213			206	647	111	8257
1904								1355	1794	5032	17	13	127			186	173	114	8811
1905								1636	2292	6939	15	11	111			258	582	206	12,050
1906								2179	2019	8647	22	12	268			230	416	212	14,005
1907								1268	477	4386	15	7	111			88	152	144	6648
1908								1523	364	5764	29	9	129			159	183	176	8316
1909								2036	653	6374	25	15	115			155	195	195	9763
1910								1923	770	6115	24	12	155			150	89	234	9472
1911								2036	978	6463	23	5	59			158	143	191	10,056
1912								1810	518	7539	18	1	103			251	409	45	10,694
1913								1461	820	5179	13	11	172			243	223	121	8233
1914								2385	1628	4434									
1915								3078	2596	2598									
1916								3435	613	895									
1917								2087	1159	1990									
1918								1445	878	1279									
1919								1097	1151	1185									
1920								765	685	1527									
1921								1984	1342	2081									
1922								982	1387	2289									
1923								915	356										
									124,193	241,224									556,813

and forty-five minutes to fire the 1,000 cartridges, and we broke between 700 and 800 clays. Each of us used three shotguns.

I have not been able to compare the remarkable shots and record bags of former times with those of today, in part because I have not been able to find reliable records for recent times.

I always wanted to put together a nine-man bird-shooting team consisting of three English, three Spanish, and three French Guns, but the idea was never realized. The shooting became terribly expensive, and it was also a question of where we would shoot. The Spanish shoots cannot be surpassed for the size of the kill, but for quality, English pheasants are hard to beat. That said, if I could have assembled my imaginary team, the Guns would have been:

From Spain: Count Bunting de Teba
                Pepe Ramón Mora-Figueroa
                Juanito Abeillo

From France: Count François de Riocour
                Claude Foussier
                Count Jean de Beaumont

From England: Sir Joe Nickerson
                Lord Tony Lambton
                Sonny Marlborough (the 11th Duke)

There may have been better Guns, but I never met them. Other outstanding Guns that I shot with would include:

Prince Alfonso Hohenlohe
Count José de Caralt
Fernando Terry
Archie Stirling
Jean d'Albert, Duke of Luynes and Chevreuze
Count André de Ganay
Henri Roussel

In an age when more and more pheasants and partridges are being reared for release, it appears likely that the foregoing records and statistics, which in most cases pertain to the shooting of wild birds, will not be surpassed.

Concluding Thoughts

My dear children, now that you have heard my story, maybe you will ask: What is the message from our father, after such an adventurous and upside-down life? I will try to answer.

What is life? You are born, and you have nothing to do with that fact. Then you study for fifteen or twenty years. Then you fall in love and eventually get married. You have some children, God willing, and you work. At the end, you see a lot of doctors. Then you die, have a funeral, and get buried or cremated. These are the basic events of life.

But you may ask, "Hey! Where and when does the fun come in?" Well, what is fun? Fun is what gives you pleasure, satisfaction, and contentment. So, what do you like? Only you can answer that question. We parents can show you where the water is, but we can't drink it for you.

I knew from a very early age what I wanted to do in life. After grade school, I knew what university I wanted to attend and what regiment I wanted to enter. After that, I planned to become a diplomat and serve my country abroad. At the age of fifty or sixty, I expected to become a member of parliament or a minister in the government. And finally, I would retire to my home in the country with grandchildren, horses, dogs, and guns.

The beginning of my life followed this program. Then I had a little problem with Joe Stalin, who robbed me of all my belongings and forced me to leave my beloved country.

You may say that all this sounds rather depressing. But, no! No! I had fun in every period of life! I thoroughly enjoyed the girls, the hunting, the country life, and even the war, if only because I survived it. What makes you happy is something that only you can know.

You have everything that anyone could ask for. All four of you are healthy, beautiful, and financially secure. Everybody likes you. Your name is known. You have an opening in every country. And from there on you have to find your own path. Do you want to work ten hours a day in an office to make money? If so, what are you going to do with your wealth? Money can buy a certain amount of freedom, safety, and contentment, but remember that some of the best things in life are free and cannot be bought at all.

I will always be grateful to my parents and grandparents for the wonderful, happy, and full life they gave me during my first twenty years. From them I learned the principles and received the qualities of character that enabled me to survive the war and its aftermath, the emigration, and my wanderings round the world.

I was twenty-two years old when I inherited our farm. That is still the only property I have ever owned, and it was promptly stolen from me. My first twenty years taught me how wonderful it is to have a real home – to be surrounded by friends and family and good will. To live like that has been my dream all through life, but it has mostly eluded me. Or maybe I was too spoiled to be satisfied with what I had.

Some suggestions: Once you have a comfortable home and a generous lifestyle, don't be greedy. There will always be a bigger private plane and a longer yacht. Learn to be satisfied with what you have, and think of others who are less fortunate. You cannot expect to receive if you do not give. And remember that to do something for someone else will give you the deepest kind of satisfaction. Try to live for your country, for your family, and for your ideals. Do what you want with the one life you have, but do *something*. This above all: stick together, help each other, and help others.

I wish you, dear Louise and the 4 P's, a free and healthy life in a comfortable home and with no serious problems.

All happiness to you! Whatever that is!

Stephaich Genealogy

József Stephaich de Nemes-Déd,
born around 1580,
represented the County of Somogy
at the coronation of Matthias II
as King of Hungary, in 1608

|

?

|

Gáspár Stephaich de Nemes-Déd,
living 1700/1730,
m. Erzse Imre

|

Márton Stephaich de Nemes-Déd,
certified his nobility in 1763,
m. Mária Koroknyai,
of a noble family

|

Miklós Stephaich de Nemes-Déd,
born in 1740,
m. Klára Toth de Felsószopor

|

Gáspár Stephaich de Nemes-Déd,
born February 11, 1773,
certified his nobility on March 18, 1828,
died October 12, 1850
m. Erzsébet Barcza de Nagyalásony

|

Pál Stephaich de Nemes-Déd,
born July 17, 1820,
died January 6, 1878,
m. Mária Thassy de Miske és Monostor
born June 7, 1830,
daughter of Károly de Thassy
and Anna Somogyi de Medgyes

Pál Stephaich de Nemes-Déd,
born April 18, 1861, died December 15, 1942,
m. Mária Gombos de Zágorhida,
born November 19, 1865, died May 12, 1916

Pál Stephaich de Nemes-Déd,
born November 26, 1887, August 26, 1966,
m. Theodóra ("Dóra") Kladnigg,
born October 31, 1894, died August 27, 1984

Pál Stephaich de Nemes-Déd,	Péter Stephaich de Nemes-Déd,	Mária ("Irmi") Stephaich de Nemes-Déd,
born July 31,1916	*born June 3, 1920,* m. Louise Eustis Hitchcock, *born January 1, 1930*	*born June 30, 1918,* m. Gyula Kacskovics de Daruvár

Peter Stephaich,	Paul Stephaich,	Peggy Stephaich,	Pauline Stephaich,
born *February 26, 1956,* m. Raquel Daher	*born* *September 13, 1958*	*born* *February 15, 1960,* m. Hon. Sebastian Guinness	*born* *January 11, 1964*

Andrea Stephaich,	Laura Stephaich,
born January 9, 1989	*born January 23, 1991*

Epilogue

It will now be in December, six years ago when Peter has left us. Or has he? His imposing figure surges into my memory every time, weekly, when I drive under the windows of the old apartment, Place des Etats-Unis. It struck me when I met him late in his life that he had a first searching glance, as if to size up your mood of the day before flashing his happy smile. He had that magic talent to make you feel good instantly because you live in a wonderful world. It signalled that you are a friend and as such, bad or unpleasant things should not intrude to spoil our meeting. And, as our meetings multiplied in the late Autumn months in 2010, he reminded me with growing insistence that we are friends, that our parents were friends, that IRMI, his sister KAC-SKOVICS and my uncle spent the awesome weeks of the Budapest siege by Russian troops, together in the winter of 1944, that we must speak of the good old days and remember . . .

Peter was 10 years my elder: in the old Hungarian tradition, this age difference imposed a hierarchic respect of him by me. Unconsciously, we applied this rule and I listened attentively as he explained to his young friend: "Sandor, you have at least 10 good years left ahead of you. You must be sure to take your full share of fun in life".

His tone reflected the stubborn trauma of Hungarians reduced to total destitution after the war, that good old times can fast be gone.

Peter was a "structurally" proud Hungarian. He came into this world one year after the abominable Traité de Versailles was signed. It stripped Hungary of three quarters of its historic territory and two thirds of its population. The pain and humiliation inflicted to the generation at the time cannot be understood by those who have not suffered from it. Families were torn apart, territories arbitrarily carved away. The loss of Big Hungary was an ulcerating sore which crowded into the school programs and dramatically infected Peter's early years, from elementary to high school. Born in the pastoral south-western corner of Hungary, cradle of centuries-old ancestral noble family, Peter had a happy, protected childhood. It was forever God's country for him. He was brought up in a profoundly affectionate family atmosphere with its strict rules and rituals of secular tradition which were gently but firmly imposed. You could enjoy yourself but your manner and bearing had to be impeccable. Parents had to be obeyed without question. Your school work had to be done at the cost of effort and diligence. Rewards for work well done were generous. The first and most prized reward was his successful initiation in hunting. His career path was carefully charted through a top university towards the elite exclusive Academy of Cavalry Regiment, the famous Huszars, the legendary, mythic horsemen: the heritage of his patriotic ancestry would thus be assured.

More than three centuries of brave defence of our Christian civilisation stands to the credit of the Huszars and the last one could not be more emblematic.

Finally, he would become a diplomat, perhaps a statesman as befits a Stephaich. The family saw in him early, the bearing, courage and mind-set to achieve his ends. The shockwave of 1929 was the first hiccup to jolt the tranquillity of the Hungarian microcosm to which he belonged. It had a sobering impact leaving many people in ruins and leaving its marks on Peter. As the environment improved, he remembered fondly the vibrancy of young Hungarians in the late thirties whose yearning for amusement, whose urgency to forget problems, to take advantage of new amenities such as automobiles, to muffle rumblings of conflicts, to live it up, prevailed.

These were the best years of his life, the unforgettable glitter of the golden thirties. Life was a carrousel of balls, dancing the Csardas to the music of the Tzigans, and the sacred hunting parties. Life was a dream, especially for the handsome ranking officer of the elite regiment of the Huszars: young Peter Stephaich. He had his time of the day.

Enchanting, glorious years soon came to a crushing end as ominous rumblings of Nazi Germany unleashed an apocalyptic carnage from which our civilisation emerged moribund. Hungarians were stripped of their properties, up to their national identity, by the inhumane bureaucracy of a monolithic communist regime. The hardship inflicted is unfathomable. Peter summed it up in a cold fury: that is how I came to lose my home, my possessions and worst of all, my beloved country. I was forced to live like an immigrant refugee for the rest of my life".

What is the direction your life will take when the one you had lies in ruins without clear horizons, with an empty pocket and stomach ? Facing up to adversity with courage and ingenuity was Peter's choice. Here is the place for an anecdote: during the course of a casual conversation, perhaps 10 years ago, Steve West, the Senior Counsel of Sullivan and Cromwell, member of the board of directors of the Swiss Helvetia Fund of which I was President, asked: "Do you happen to know a countryman of yours called Peter Stephaich ?" As I acknowledged, he said: "He was a cowhand on the Jersey estate of my neighbour Reeve Schley who told me he was a Hungarian nobleman with immaculate manners. Did he ever know and do his job!" Peter knew how to leave a lasting mark. Incidentally, Paul Soros was another neighbour of Schley.

But another ideal remained for Peter to be fulfilled: to recreate the lifestyle he knew in his youth, because he was clearly also a "structurally" fun-loving, "bon-vivant". For doing so, he had ingrained attributes and requisites. He had a natural ease and fluidity in his communication manner. Perfect grooming, a sense for gallantry, an affable approach and the right touch of authority to make his point. So many qualities he could employ skilfully. His fun loving penchant was widely recognised and appreciated because the fun he created was generously shared with friends around him. As the world was his oyster, he made friends everywhere. Jay Mellon so rightly detailed this feature in the foreword of "The Last Huszars": in fact, Peter succeeded in making an art of "L'Art de Vivre" to which this book is paying resounding tribute.

As it is explained therein, he had a phenomenal embrace of the hunting universe with its actors worldwide, its rituals, its elegance and its gripping traditions.

Hunting was part of country life throughout Europe. He had a strong loving and protective respect for nature, its wildlife and the animal world: big game killing and bird shooting it was a paramount importance for him that the practice of age old traditions of rules and disciplines be strictly obeyed.

It took me just a few minutes to walk up to Peter's flat from mine. I was fond of him and felt it an honor in some ways to be received by the rare gentleman of old times. His last comments had his bias that the too important things in life should be taken light heartedly and simply. I had the certainty that he loved you all deeply and dearly, more than he would say. The last time I went to Clinique Bizet, he would return home two days later when we would meet.

I miss him.

Alexandre de Takacsy

www.ingramcontent.com/pod-product-compliance
Ingram Content Group UK Ltd.
Pitfield, Milton Keynes, MK11 3LW, UK
UKHW021352310325
5245UKWH00026B/276